NATIONAL SECURITY
MANAGEMENT

GLOBAL
PSYCHOLOGICAL
CONFLICT

Edited by

Ralph Sanders
Fred R. Brown

INDUSTRIAL COLLEGE OF THE ARMED FORCES
WASHINGTON, D.C.
1961

INDUSTRIAL COLLEGE OF THE ARMED FORCES
Washington, D.C.

AUGUST SCHOMBURG, Lt. Gen., USA
Commandant

WILLIAM S. STEELE, Major Gen., USAF
Deputy Commandant

J. E. REHLER, Captain, USN
Director, Correspondence School

———

———

FOREWORD

This volume is the product of an effort to portray current analytical thought concerning the psychological conflict between the East and the West. An earlier work entitled *Psychological Aspects of Global Conflict*, edited by Dr. Benjamin H. Williams, had served a similar purpose. The present text includes seven new chapters in addition to two retained from the previous volume.

With the growing importance of psychological conflict in the cold war, the editors have deemed it advisable to give particular attention to pertinent operational and organizational aspects of the continuing struggle. They have also strived to allow for a variety of points of view and interpretations in dealing with a subject having many admittedly controversial and uncertain aspects. Accordingly, the reader will need to evaluate and to reconcile those differences that inevitably crop up in a compilation of current thought on psychological conflict.

The Industrial College of the Armed Forces is indebted to the contributors to this volume and to the publishers who kindly consented to the use of their copyrighted materials.

Ralph Sanders
Fred R. Brown

Industrial College of the Armed Forces
Washington, D.C.
1 September 1961

CONTENTS

ILLUSTRATIONS

INTRODUCTION

The celebrated Chinese, Sun Tzu, writing on military affairs in the Fifth Century B.C., in his *The Book of War*, stressed the importance of destroying the enemy's will to fight through such means as surprise and noise. This ancient Chinese suggested beacons and drums in night fighting, using great numbers of banners in day fighting, and spreading tales of treachery of trusted leaders and their associations with enemy leaders. All this was calculated to destroy the enemy's will to resist with minimum cost to one's own fighting capacity. Some 2500 years later, Sun Tzu's doctrines have come back to haunt mankind. The Sino-Soviet bloc, aiming to defeat the West with minimum cost to itself, and bidding to dominate the world, has refined Sun Tzu's simple prescriptions into a fine art.

This volume provides a concise treatment of the psychological aspects of the global conflict. Mainly, it offers discussions of the efforts to direct and sway the attitudes considered relevant in the cold war. Conversely, it does not examine in any detail specific psychological techniques and devices used in open warfare. Its analyses deal with Communist and Free World motivations and the methods employed to influence the minds of men.

The economics of national security can be better understood through familiarizing oneself with the international aspects of mobilizing all resources to meet the Communist menace. And, as we shall see, the manner in which we use our resources undoubtedly has a great influence on the thinking of millions of people throughout the world. The thoughts and attitudes of these millions are of paramount significance since the mind is one of the most important battlegrounds of the cold war. Consequently, it is important to learn the ideology advocated by each side as well as the respective approaches to and operational techniques of psychological conflict. Chapter I reviews the role of ideology in this conflict, its importance, and its relation to national power.

Psychological operations are not formulated or executed in a vacuum; they need direction and organization. There must be a policymaking apparatus and an implementation mechanism, both under capable leadership. Since psychological factors influence or are influenced by a multitude of actions, ranging over the entire spectrum of national life, governments must coordinate, at least, the major plans and operations of their psychological efforts. Chapters II and III examine the organization of the psychological activities of the Soviet Union and the United States. The next two chapters investigate the views of the chief contenders in the psychological battle and their attitudes toward psychological strategy.

Chapter VI is concerned with the use of the language tool in the struggle for men's minds. The message is often clothed in semantic apparel designed to be attractive, and preferably, seductive. The bulk of chapter VI examines how the Soviets manipulate words to serve their psychological ends.

Chapters VII and VIII examine the psychological considerations in our conduct of foreign relations in the cold war. The first of these chapters discusses the importance of human reactions and behavior as they relate to general foreign policy; the second covers the psychological factors underlying the economics of the cold war. The West now faces a growing Communist economic offensive in many parts of the world. There is no doubt that Russia intends to reap more than just the gratitude of underdeveloped peoples for the aid it provides; in fact, it seeks a psychological and political payoff. By highlighting the psychological aspects of this economic conflict, the chapter should aid the student to understand a very important international phase of the economics of national security.

The last chapter summarizes the material of the previous chapters, relating them to the deeper psychological characteristics of contemporary societies. It examines how the Communists exploit personal and group insecurity so prevalent in today's complex world to serve their own ends. Technology, especially sophisticated weaponry, increasingly prompts irrational behavior from which the Communist can profit. It is concluded that there is a need for an understanding of these deeper psychological functions by the Free World.

I
IDEOLOGICAL CONFLICT AND THE STRUGGLE FOR POWER [1]

The special subject of this chapter is ideological conflict—the kind of situation that arises when two nations confront each other with very different ideas about what governments ought to be or do, as is the case today between the United States and Russia. But this special subject is part of a larger subject to which the present volume is devoted—the ideological or psychological factor in national power and its relation to non-ideological or material factors. By psychological factors are meant such things as people's thoughts and feelings, their beliefs and theories, their conceptions of right and wrong, their aims and purposes and ideals—what is called in general their "minds" or their "philosophy." By material factors are meant such things as natural resources, technology, transportation, the capacity to produce all kinds of goods that affect their power in international politics. The more general subject raises questions such as these: Of the two kinds of factors, which has the greater weight? In forecasting what a government will probably do, or in estimating what it will be able to do, should a policymaker rely more on one than on the other? Is his problem solved merely by assuming that politics is a struggle for power and that governments will use all the power they can muster? How can he use the less tangible psychological factors to keep up morale on his own side or to weaken an opponent? The more special subject includes questions like these: When two peoples with conflicting ideologies confront one another, what may be expected to happen? Must the conflict of ideas end in a conflict of force? Or can it be controlled, and if so how can a policymaker best contribute to this result? The present chapter will present some general considerations bearing on both classes of question.

Let me begin by telling an experience that first brought vividly to my mind the great weight that ideological factors have in any attempt to influence people's action. A good many years ago I attended a conference between several scientists who had been called as consultants to advise a foreign government on modernizing its agricultural production, specifically its corn crop. This was before

---

[1] Chapter I was contributed by the late Dr. George H. Sabine, Professor of Philosophy, Cornell University, Ithaca, New York, to the earlier volume of 1955. It has been retained in this compilation because of its penetrating analysis of the subject.

the days of point 4 and foreign aid, but the problems were the same as these later programs have always had to meet. The principal speaker was an expert on soils, an excellent scientist but also a man of broad practical experience and wisdom. What he said was in substance this. The scientific problem is easy. So far as it is a question of things like fertilizer or seed corn, we can tell them in half an hour what needs to be done to increase their yield. But let me see you persuade a population of peasant farmers to do it! And he told a story, which may or may not have been literally true, about an agricultural project somewhere in Africa to induce the natives to adopt modern methods of tillage. The idea was to set up pilot farms to show by example how yields really could be increased. The natives learned, but what they learned was not what was desired or expected. They killed the farmer with the best model farm, cut his body into pieces, and buried the pieces in the less productive fields! Their idea was that his "power" would thus be imparted to the soil. To their way of thinking the answer was not scientific agriculture but magic.

The point of the story is this. Making a policy or laying down a line of strategy, or administering the process of putting a policy into effect, is essentially an effort to predict what people will do, individually or in the mass, and to direct their behavior toward a desired end. Such an effort must meet psychological or ideological factors. There are ideological factors on all sides of it, since having an ideology is a universal trait of human nature. Whether a policymaker or an administrator is thinking of an opponent, or an ally, or of his own staff, he needs to keep in mind the fact that they will all have their own ways of looking at things which will affect what they will probably do and indeed what they can do. Perhaps the hardest thing to keep in mind is that one's own people has its ideology just as other peoples have theirs, for everyone is inclined to think that his own way of looking at things is just the "natural" way, or the way of all right-thinking people. In fact, a successful administrator, in his choice of subordinates or in keeping up morale, has to recognize that his staff, both individually and as a group, can react to a situation only through their own psychological and ideological makeup, that it is bad administration to expect them to do what they won't or can't do, and that it is still worse administration to get angry because they don't do it. The policymaker in the field of foreign relations, who has to calculate on the cooperation of his allies or estimate the probable moves of an opponent, is in the same position. He has to take account of psychological or ideological factors, just as he has to take account of material factors, if he is to know what he can reasonably expect, or what he can persuade or even force people to do in a given situation.

In general, the view presented in this chapter is as follows: Intelligent policy-making, in taking account of psychological and ideological factors, has to think of them in broadly the same way as it thinks of nonpsychological or material factors. It has to recognize their existence, to understand how they work, to realize that they can never be safely ignored or by-passed, and that there is no sense in trying to argue them out of existence because they seem to be unreasonable or stupid. As in dealing with material forces, policymaking must, in the case of nonmaterial forces, take advantage of the opportunities offered and avoid the obstacles presented, which is the definition of intelligence in either area. Some such point of view is implied by the very existence of a volume dealing with the psychological aspects of national strategy. But doing the thing is not as simple as it sounds when you say it. Everybody's mind is filled up with *cliches* and commonsense rules about human nature and the way it acts or ought to act, and these are usually picked up by the simplest and most uncritical kind of observation. If a person is sufficiently inexperienced, he will assume that human nature is always and everywhere like what he finds it, or imagines it to be, at home, and that all sorts of people are influenced by the same motives and arguments. And this just is not true. The point of view here presented requires a kind of respect for facts, which is the essence of all scientific work, and it implies the use of special knowledge gained by social psychologists, anthropologists, and historians from observations as carefully controlled as those which make an engineer an expert in technology. The policymaker or the administrator has to depend on knowledge got from both kinds of specialty. With respect to the ideological or psychological factors in administrative problems, the point of view presented in this chapter was worked out in detail in Alexander Leighton's *The Governing of Men*,[2] which brought both psychology and anthropology to bear on analyzing a peculiarly difficult situation in the last war. In respect to foreign affairs the point of view of this chapter has much in common with the argument of George F. Kennan's *American Diplomacy*,[3] 1900–50 and with the articles which Mr. Kennan published earlier in the journal *Foreign Affairs*. His thesis was that diplomacy has to deal realistically and understandingly, not emotionally, with relationships of power between nations considered as human forces, and that these forces may be partly stabilized but cannot be repressed.

IDEOLOGY AND THE DRIVE FOR POWER

The discussion of this question has been beset by two kinds of oversimplification. The first of these lies in the supposition, perhaps most often made by practical men who deal with things rather than people, that there must be some blanket motive, common to human

---

[2] Alexander H. Leighton, *The Governing of Men*, Princeton, Princeton Univ. Press, 1946.
[3] George F. Kennan, *American Diplomacy*, Chicago, Univ. of Chicago Press, 1951.

nature, that will give the key once for all to people's behavior. The word "ideology" and perhaps the word "idea" itself often suggest something insubstantial as compared with a hard material fact, something not quite real or something that might easily be changed. A person who looks at ideology in this light is likely to conclude that feelings, hopes, theories, or moral and religious beliefs are a kind of veneer, perhaps even camouflage, spread over some underlying force like self-interest or the drive for power that really explains what people do. This amounts to supposing that if you know the sources of power that a government has at its disposal, you can infer what its policy will be in actual cases. The opposite kind of oversimplification lies in the supposition, perhaps more often made by philosophers, that people as a rule behave logically, so that if you know their ideas and purposes, or in general their "philosophy," you can infer what they will do. This view assumes that an ideology is a consistent system of propositions, like a scientific theory, and that people's behavior follows from it. Thus, for example, it is often said that communism simply puts in practice the principles of Marx's philosophy.

The essence of what follows is that neither of these oversimplified ways of looking at people is literally true, though there is some truth in each of them, and that either would be misleading if it were followed implicitly. With respect to the first, it is quite true that policies revolve around great natural forces like supplies of raw materials, geographical features that obstruct or facilitate transportation, and the technology that utilizes raw materials to produce goods. It is elementary to say that a policymaker cannot afford to overlook facts like these, but to say that by knowing them he knows what will happen in a concrete political situation is a plain error. The notion that human behavior can be fully explained by physical environment is really a myth. But it is equally a myth to say that behavior can be logically deduced from a philosophy; no nation is that logical and no philosophy is that detailed. It is quite true that the way a society develops can be influenced by highly speculative theories or even by illusions, but it is never fully determined by them. In the example mentioned, that of communism, innumerable important changes in Marx's theories and in their own ideology were forced on both Lenin and Stalin by circumstances which they could not control. This was shown in detail by Barrington Moore in his *Soviet Politics* [4] which uses the case of Russia to illustrate "the role of ideas in social change." Moore's conclusions are confirmed by Merle Fainsod's *How Russia is Ruled* [5] which describes the program of the Bolshevik Party in 1917 as "an ambivalent juxtaposition of long-term expedients." But though the

[4] Barrington Moore, *Soviet Politics*, Cambridge, Harvard Univ. Press, 1950.
[5] Merle Fainsod, *How Russia Is Ruled*, Cambridge, Harvard Univ. Press, 1953.

6

ideology of communism was repeatedly amended, and often for the purpose of consolidating the Party's power, this dilemma—the dilemma of power, as Moore calls it—led always to modifying the ideology rather than to abandoning it. As Mr. Kennan says, "Nothing has been officially junked."

To put the matter positively, the view here presented is two-sided. Many of the ideas that people entertain have little or no scientific standing and some of them may be not only speculative or mythological but even downright illusory, yet these may easily affect their behavior and so need to be taken into account by a policymaker or an administrator. But ideas never operate in a vacuum. The person who holds them is always likely to encounter situations that are recalcitrant. A Communist finds, for example, that the world revolution just does not occur on schedule, or a line of action indicated by some ideological preferences turns out to be incompatible with some other preferences, and a choice has to be made. An ideology is always likely to be confronted by situations that it has to deal with but that it cannot deal with in the way it would prefer, or that would be most in accord with its theories and presuppositions. In such cases it adapts itself to obstacles, but as a rule it modifies its ideas or postpones their accomplishment rather than abandons them. It is flexible in meeting obstacles, and often it is versatile enough to have more than one way to meet them. From the point of view of logic, an ideology is rather a loose-jointed kind of thing. It is a product partly of choices and preferences, of preconceived theories and their implications, but also of trial and error, of experimentation, and even of improvisation, because it continually meets conditions that it cannot control and whose outcome it cannot accurately foresee.

In order to make this conclusion clearer I shall state very briefly and abstractly what sort of thing an ideology is. Then I shall illustrate with some examples how ideologies do in fact influence policymaking and also how they are modified when they encounter circumstances which they cannot control.

An ideology is a highly variegated and complicated body of beliefs, hopes, aspirations, convictions about good and bad, preferences about what is beautiful or ugly, theories and myths about the way things have happened or ought to happen, ritualistic and religious observances, notions of good form, or precedence and leadership, of prestige and deference. Ideologies are further complicated by the fact that they can be elaborately subdivided into special ideologies of the classes or the parts of the society that possess them. The ideology of the Russian peasant, for example, is far different from that of the industrial worker, yet both are Russians.

There are three characteristics of an ideology that need to be grasped in order to understand the kind of thing it is. First, an ideology no doubt depends in a broad sense on the experience of the people who hold it; it has been bred in them by their manner of life and may not be easily comprehensible to people with a different way of living. But large parts of it are not amenable to proof and have not been formed by examining evidence. It is not irrational but large parts of it are nonrational, both in the sense that it has not been proved and also because much of it is the sort of thing that cannot be proved. Many of its less tangible meanings, which may also be its most effective meanings, are carried merely in the subtle connotations of the language that its people use. Consider, for example, the political and moral meanings conveyed by the English word "freedom," and the emotional drive that these meanings carry; then reflect on the difficulty of imparting these meanings to a person whose language has no equivalent word. There are many such languages in the world.

Second, though an ideology is patterned in such a way that its parts go together and are internally related—as a whole it amounts to what we vaguely call "a way of life"—it is not logically or systematically interconnected in such a way that it may not include beliefs that on occasion are at odds with one another. On the contrary, beliefs and practices frequently get crossways of one another in such a way that they have to be readjusted, or one has to be selected and the other disregarded for the time being. A large-scale example, and one of enormous importance in international politics, is the relation between communism and nationalism. In theory they always were, and still are, incompatible, since communism professes to be a movement of the working people of all countries. Yet during the German invasion Russian patriotism was probably the most powerful support of Russian morale, and the spread of communism in Asia is closely connected with its ability to pose as an exponent of nationalism against colonialism.

Third, the various elements of an ideology are of widely different degrees of importance. They range all the way from trivial matters of habit that are no more than conventional good form up to the kind of convictions that men will fight and die for. Moreover, this body of practices and beliefs is carried and transmitted by tradition; every generation learns it anew. Consequently some parts of it are new; some are obsolete and obsolescent and may be relatively disregarded. But such old-fashioned ways are not disregarded except as they die away with time. They are often reserved for another occasion and may be revived or readapted. An ideology is an arsenal that contains more weapons than are used at any one time.

I come now to the illustrations. The proposition to be illustrated is twofold, that a body of beliefs such as has been described does in fact influence policy, but also that in its operation it encounters conditions that may reflect it very far from any preconceived idea of its chosen course. These inescapable conditions, however, do not in any precise sense "cause" the policy; they force it rather to adapt itself, or modify its course, in ways that were not foreseen but which remain more or less consistent with purposes and goals set by the ideology. If a figure of speech will make the matter clearer, an ideology is like a very flexible medium, a river for example, that can flow round an obstacle and yet keep a continuous course. The illustrations will be drawn from Russian Marxism, partly because the conflict of Russian with American ideology is the reason for this book but also because the studies, already mentioned, by Barrington Moore and Merle Fainsod have carefully analyzed the interplay of ideological and non-ideological factors in Russian policy since 1917. This policy will be seen, as Mr. Kennan has said, to have been the "product of ideology and circumstance."

In 1917, on the eve of the Communist revolution, Lenin wrote the little pamphlet entitled *State and Revolution*, which will probably stand as the authoritative ideological statement of the aims and presumptions with which the Bolshevik Party took power. In it he outlined what he then imagined a Socialist society would be like. He fancied in the first place that capitalist technology had already reduced the functions of management in industry to routine operations comparable with recordkeeping, checking, and filing: "has simplified the functions of accounting and control, and has reduced them to such comparatively simple processes as to be within the reach of any literate person." From this he deduced in the second place that in a Socialist society authority and management would be widely shared and that pay could be equalized at a rate sufficient to employ clerks having the qualifications mentioned. This was typical ideological forecast of policy, "nebulous, visionary, and impractical," as Mr. Kennan calls it. It depended in part on the Marxian dogma that capitalist management renders itself progressively superfluous and in part on the hope that a Socialist society could quite easily make men equal in money and power.

This pleasant vision lasted less than six months. Before the end of that time Lenin had discovered that "the art of administration is not an art that one is born to." Attempts to do more or less the sort of thing pictured in *State and Revolution* resulted in a catastrophic decline of production both in industry and agriculture, and this in turn produced a degree of misery and discontent that threatened to drive his party out of power. By 1921, under the threat of the Kronstadt Rebellion, Lenin had switched to the New Economic Policy. Over a period of twenty years following the Revolution, Russian industry was forced to adopt policies of management, of accounting, of incentives by wage differentials, and of recruiting and dis-

9

ciplining its labor force which were broadly similar to those in a capitalist economy and which, by the use of coercion and forced labor, were in practice vastly more oppressive. The initial ideal of equality had been changed to what Moore calls "organized inequality"—an acceptance of the fact that some differences of pay, of rank, of prestige, and of authority are conditions without which an industrial technology cannot be made to work. In short, any system of large-scale industrial production has some properties of its own quite independent of ideology, and these impose necessities, or limit possibilities, whatever the ideology may be. The same conclusion could be equally well illustrated if an example not drawn from industry were chosen. Early Communist attempts to remake the family ended in an amount of juvenile delinquency that finally produced divorce laws more stringent that those of most American states.

Next, however, I wish to rule out any hasty conclusion that perhaps the ideology did not count at all, to show that the ideology was in some respects decisive even though it was not all-powerful, so that neglecting it would have led to very erroneous predictions. Lenin's switch to the New Economic Policy undoubtedly compromised his Communist principles, as he understood them, but it was successful in bringing a considerable upswing of production. The result would probably have convinced most persons not saturated with Marxism that a Communist economy was simply impossible. In fact Western economists often predicted that the New Economic Policy was a step toward abandoning communism altogether and that the Russian economy would become more and more capitalistic. Something of the sort probably would have happened if the rulers of Russia could have entertained the ideology of a free-enterprise economy. They would have been more ready to believe that the switch from communism was inevitable and depended on a "natural" or normal property of any economic system. Another possibility, perhaps even more obvious in a country overwhelmingly agricultural, with a population more than 80 percent peasant, might have been to turn policy toward satisfying the demands of the peasantry. Obviously, neither of these courses was chosen. Marxian ideology had always been committed to the belief that a modern nation must be industrial—an opinion that was reenforced by realistic ambitions for military power—and under the circumstances the accumulation of industrial capital meant exploitation of the peasants. But even so the conclusion was not simply a deduction from Marxian principles. The whole decade of the 1920's was filled with bitter controversies in the Russian Communist Party about how fast industrialization should go and how it might be achieved within a system that should be at once Communist and viable. The answer was reached by a combination of ideological aims and opportunist experimentation in the Five Year Plans and the consolidation of Stalin's power. The expectations with which the experiments were started often proved false, some practices of capitalist management had to be adopted, but the system evolved was, broadly speaking, Communist. The Second World War proved it to be viable.

This combination of ideological and nonideological factors can be well illustrated in one of the critical developments of the policy—the enforced collectivization of agriculture. For anyone who considers agricultural production from the standpoint of an individualist economy, collectivization was full of paradoxes. Ostensibly its purpose was to increase output, but it liquidated the better-to-do farmers, with the larger holdings of land, and with a larger yield per unit than the average. In short, it tried to increase production by scrapping the most productive parts of the existing system. Actually several purposes cooperated in the policy of collectivization. No matter what ideology prevailed industrializing the country would have changed radically the system of peasant agriculture that existed in Russia, not only to increase production but also to modernize agricultural technology and free manpower for industry. From a merely administrative standpoint it was easier to deal with a few collective farms than with millions of peasant farmers. It was also believed that the growth of a class of capitalist farm-owners would be incompatible with a planned Socialist industrial system and would jeopardize the retention of power by a party committed to that system. Behind all these considerations there was a powerful ideological bias in favor of a collective rather than an individual economy, the belief that nothing else was consistent with Marxism and that Marxism was the inevitable "wave of the future." As a matter of fact a mixed economy, combining Socialist and individualist features, was probably not impossible and may yet indicate the direction in which collectivized agriculture will move, but for the time being the Marxian bias foreclosed experiments along that line and imposed its pattern on the policy. A prediction that neglected the ideology would have been wide of the mark but the actual process could never have been deduced merely from the philosophical principles of Marxism.

Throughout all the twists and turns of policy since the Revolution of 1917 there was, of course, one motive that remained consistent—the determination of the Bolshevik leadership to retain and consolidate its power. In the outcome this determination, in the words of Professor Fainsod, "dwarfed all other objectives" and confronted the Party with "the tragedy of unintended consequences," for its avowed purposes had to be constantly postponed or abandoned in "a complex struggle to master the recalcitrant realities" of its actual situation. Establishing and extending its power was the one principle that the Party always regarded as axiomatic, and it was this which led it toward constantly growing practices of repression at home and aggression abroad. But this pursuit of power was not independent of ideology. It was the dogmatism of Marx's philosophy, made vastly more dogmatic by Lenin, that engendered the belief that there can never be more than one right belief and that any dissent whatever is a threat to stable government. It was Marxian ideology rather than the actual facts that induced in the Bolshevik leadership the belief that the world is its enemy and that international capitalism is a menace which justifies terrorism at home and aggression abroad. The desire for power is no doubt a powerful human motive but it is not self-explanatory. It does not enable one to predict the course a government will adopt to further its power or what it will use its power to accomplish.

To sum up, the relation between ideological and nonideological factors in policymaking is somewhat as follows: Both kinds of factors are always present, both always have an effect upon the result, and both are likely to lead to unforseen consequences. Any policy that is at all far-reaching will encounter conditions that impose some elements of the solution. There are always large elements of trial and error, and experiments react on the ideological goals that set the policy. Some purposes are abandoned, some are postponed, and some are amended. But there are usually more ways than one of moving toward a general result. Ideological aims persist in modified form and continue to affect the experiments. The human being just does not exist who can get wholly outside the intellectual and moral tradition in which his mind has for years been steeped, and this is as true of persons who direct governments as it is of other persons. The kind of question they will ask, the kind of experiment they will try, the way they will meet the necessities of a situation, the kind of purpose for which they use their power, will all be partly determined by ideological factors—by theories and by moral or religious or even by mythological beliefs. Suppose you were to try in imagination this experiment: Visualize the problems that a Russian government faced between 1921 and 1936; then ask yourself how a government composed of American or English liberals would have tried to meet them, in comparison with the way in which Russian Marxists did try to meet them. The answer is an index of in the influence of ideology. It is pretty certain that the answer will agree substantially with Barrington Moore's: "Althought Stalin's solutions to the problems he faced have a highly eclectic character, his borrowings were all drafts upon the treasury of Marxist intellectual tradition." [6]

Certain conclusions follow which have practical importance for anyone who has the responsibility for laying down the lines of national strategy and for predicting the policy that another government will adopt.

---

[6] Moore, *op. cit.*, p. 114.

First, it follows that ideological factors cannot be safely neglected, any more than physical or technological factors can. A prediction based on either one to the exclusion of the other will probably be wrong, or at least will be less exact than it might have been. Unavoidable conditions have to be met but ideological factors largely determine how a government will try to meet them and indeed how it can meet them. And as was said at the start, there is always ideology on both sides. A realistic policymaker can no more neglect the ideology of his own people or his own staff than he can neglect that of his opponent. In good administration and good strategy there is an element of detachment and of understanding, a little like the way in which a historian looks at a foreign culture. Perhaps this is a reason why historical reading has always been a staple with statesmen.

Second, the ideological factors in any important situation are very complex and the parts are not always rigidly consistent with one another. "The Marxist intellectual tradition" mentioned by Mr. Moore had been a matter of philosophical dispute for seventy-five years before the Russians tried to put it in practice. A vast literature, and continuous verbal discussion and propaganda, had grown up around every question, and these disputes continued among Russian Marxists as long as there was any freedom of discussion. The tradition was literally a "treasury" which might honor very different "drafts." Even among those who professed the most complete acceptance of Marxian principles there was never close agreement about what the principles exactly meant in practice. Characteristically an ideology is not exact in the sense that it rigidly implies detailed consequences. Rather, it suggests a range of possibilities and enjoins a kind of attitude.

Third, an ideology does not characteristically provide unambiguous rules of behavior or policy but rather alternatives from which a selection can be made as circumstances require. For example: Does Marxism imply that a world revolution is imminent within a fairly short time or does it imply that socialism is possible for a fairly long time in one country? Will a Marxist, then, follow a policy aimed at fomenting revolution in foreign countries or will he adopt the policy of a popular front based on the coexistence of capitalism and communism? And will he treat the Communist parties of other countries as ideological brothers or will he treat them as expendable for the benefit of the "Socialist homeland"? Everybody knows that Russian Marxists have done both, and have justified both with Marxist arguments. This sort of two-faced argument may, of course, be merely hypocritical, and it is quite certain that the Party's propaganda machine will take either side quite cynically. But in truth the logic is about equally good, or bad, in either case, for Marxism as a system is loose-jointed enough to support either conclusion according to circumstances. Characterically, there are two strings to the ideological bow. It is more likely to suggest a range of ideas and concepts within which a particular case may fall than a single rule under which it must fall. An understanding of the ideology may enable a policy-maker to grasp the several possibilities, to weigh the probability of one against the other, and to keep his own policy on balance whichever actually develops.

Fourth, an ideology is filled with reserved or unfulfilled beliefs and suggestions for behavior that are inactive at a given time, or are taken as not quite literal, but which certainly are not abandoned and are quite capable of coming to life. In general, postponement is more characteristic of ideological hopes and beliefs than abandonment. People say, perhaps, that "the time is not ripe," or "the present is not the best time," and yet they may still believe that the postponed line of action is sound and right. It may still express a valued part of the ideological faith and on another occasion it may be revived in full vigor. Certainly Marxism has always included remote goals of this sort—glittering generalities like the "classless society." or an economy in which every man receives the full value of his labor, or a brotherhood in which exploitation never occurs. Much of its appeal has consisted in holding up utopian ideals such as these before peoples that have real grievances but have little or no experience of the practical difficulty of improving their economic or political situation. These ideals are never "officially scrapped," even when they are neglected in practice. They are postponed to an indefinite future. But it would be risky to overlook the powerful impact that such ideas may carry. An imaginative appreciation of the attitudes and feelings that such beliefs engender may be an important factor in predicting a people's reactions.

IDEOLOGICAL CONFLICTS AND THEIR CONTROL

The purpose of considering these general characteristics of ideology has been to ask what light they throw on the control of ideological conflicts. When differing ideologies stand sharply in opposition to one another, what can a policymaker do to prevent the opposition from developing into war? As was said at the beginning of this chapter, this is the kind of situation that now confronts American diplomacy in its relations with Russia, and the whole Western world in its relations with communism. There is no sound reason to hope that this conflict will soon disappear. Former President Eisenhower has said, "We live not in a year, not in a decade, but in an age of peril." No responsible American statesman doubts that this age of peril must not, unless as an unescapable disaster, be allowed to end in armed conflict. For after an experience of two world wars, no reasonable man can believe that a third war, even with the most complete military victory, could be anything but a disaster. The problem of national strategy, however, is not exhausted in the conflict between the two great ideologies of democracy and communism. A democratic front is dependent on an effective alliance of many nations which, though they agree in not being Communist, are still very different. Each has its own practices and beliefs which will have to be respected if they are to be combined in a smoothly working policy of voluntary cooperation. The role of the United States as the most powerful member of a democratic alliance is not consistent with the kind of coercive policy that Russia can follow toward her satellite states, and in fact such a policy is impossible. For the United States, therefore, in relation both to Russia and to its allies, control of the conflict depends on successful negotiation, and force has to figure as a supplement to negotiation.

In this part of the chapter as in the first I shall begin with some general considerations related to the nature of ideology and shall conclude with some special considerations that arise from the ideology of communism. The latter will serve as illustrations of the former.

Obviously, it would be quite inconsistent with what has been said in the first part of this chapter to pretend that there is any simple formula for composing ideological conflicts or any infallible rule for bringing peoples with different ideologies into an agreement that makes armed conflict impossible. The assumption throughout has been that policy can best be made by taking a rational attitude toward problems of human relationship, by treating them with understanding, by avoiding the obstacles they set, and by taking advantage of the opportunities they offer. This implies that there can be no rule of thumb which guarantees success in advance, that particular situations have to be taken on their merits, and that a policy has to be adapted to the ideology with which it has to deal. It implies also that, in general, policymaking moves in the realm of probability rather than certainty. This attitude calls for a high level of intelligence and self-restraint both in the policymaker and in a society that makes its policy in this way. There is a normal human desire for certainty and an impatience with uncertainty, especially in situations that are both long continued and dangerous. And there is a tendency, when policies fail to work out, to jump to the conclusion that somebody has been stupid or disloyal. This in turn tends to undermine morale and the mutual confidence on which democratic cooperation depends. Communism, indeed, can hold out the belief that its success is inevitable, that its policies are always sure to be right, but this is because communism fosters the myth that its leaders are infallible. Democracy requires a more mature intellectual outlook, the power to depend on reason rather than on magic.

It follows also that, on a rational assessment of the international situation, ideological conflicts have to be taken as inevitable and in any absolute sense irremovable. Perhaps the hardest fact that every ideology faces is the necessity of living with other ideologies. This will be true whether the problem is one of cooperating with an ally or containing an opponent. It is probably true that no two great powers have ever cooperated more effectively than Great Britain and the United States, and it is probably true also that no two are closer together in fundamental outlook and purpose. Yet this cooperation has never been automatic or of such a sort that misunderstandings did not occur. No progress of international organization can be expected to alter the situation very materially, for organization is a way of dealing with differences, not of abolishing them. If the United Nations succeeded beyond anybody's present hopes, there would still be differences of national interest and of national ideology that nothing on earth could conjure out of existence. If international organization settles down, as it has in the past, into a new balance of power, that balance will have to be maintained by the combined action of nations with very different ideologies. And if worst comes to worst and a third world war ensues, even the most sweeping military victory will not destroy the conquered ideology. At most a victory might, under proper circumstances, result in changing some features of that ideology; American policy in Europe is now banking on the hope that this will be the result of the victory over Germany in 1945. People naturally like to believe that wars have a happy ending, but as Mr. Kennan has said, wars are more likely to begin something than to end something. The only way literally to end an ideology would be to exterminate the people who hold it.

It is a sound principle of military strategy that victory consists in accomplishing your objectives. This implies that objectives are limited, that their nature is precisely known and understood, and that the means to accomplish them are used with a clear perception of their bearing on the end in view. The point of view developed in this chapter assumes that the same principle applies to policymaking in the larger sphere of international relationships, and to political as well as military objectives. In dealing with other nations the policymaker has to take the circumstances, the conditions of power, the ideologies that are factors in power and its exercise, and even personalities pretty much as he finds them, and he has to handle them with the means at his disposal, whether the latter are means of persuasion or of coercion. As a general rule, if he is confronted with an attitude or a tradition or an aspiration shared by a whole people, he cannot hope to change these large ideological factors very much in any short time, and it is doubtful whether by coercion he can change them at all. Still less is it likely that he can change them by scolding, by telling people how wicked or unreasonable they are, or by assuming that his own policy is righteous while all others are bad. His policy will not succeed by reason of its abstract goodness, even though it needs to have moral qualities of fairness and detachment from a single national interest. A foreign policy with limited objectives is not a way of assigning demerit but of finding workable solutions to problems that upset the international stability of a world that must include peoples with very different ways of life in constantly changing relationships.

A policy of limited objectives is one also that adapts itself to the situation which in any given case confronts it. It is obvious that different ideologies put very different limits on a policy of conciliation, or put different obstacles in its way, or offer different opportunities that can be taken advantage of to make the policy succeed. It is for this reason that a policymaker who aims to control ideological conflicts needs to get a clear picture of the way things look from the standpoint of the people he has to deal with, whether as an ally or as an opponent. Generally speaking, every ideology has to make its adjustments and its concessions in its own way, and if it is to be persuaded to make them peaceably, it has to be approached in ways that it understands and with arguments that appear to it to carry weight. A policy to control ideological conflict will not succeed by virtue of its abstract reasonableness. Such conflicts are not typically resolved by refuting one and proving the other, as if ideologies were scientific theories, for all peoples (including ourselves) believe a great many things they cannot prove. In fact, a head-on argumentative attack on a dogma is less likely to convince a true believer than to harden him in his belief and make him more rigidly dogmatic in affirming it and acting on it. Attack often consolidates the opposition. In the interests of peace some questions are best answered by not being asked. A policy of conciliation has to be one of temporizing, which is a very different thing from appeasing or vacillating. It aims to show the kind of firm front that discourages aggression, while at the same time it prevents affairs from getting into the position of irreconcilable opposition. This is a job that has continually to be worked at and is never done.

These generalities will be clearer if they are considered in the light of the situation which the ideology of communism now presents to the foreign policy of the United States.

It is evident that Marxism, and especially the version of Marxism adopted by Lenin, puts a formidable obstacle in the way of peaceful agreement by its concept of the class-struggle. This dogma—for it is a dogma rather than an observation of fact—is conceived by Communists to express a fundamental law of all politics, so long as the difference between communism and capitalism persists, and one that neither intention nor desire nor voluntary act can alter. At the level of international relations this law implies that all governments must divide into capitalist or Communist, and that between the two classes there can never be any sincere presumption of a permanent community of interests. The antagonism between them is ineradicable; it can never end except with the domination of one system or the other, and ultimately, as Communists believe, with the predestined victory of communism. From this point of view politics is essentially war, and Communists habitually use military metaphors to describe it; peacetime politics is the continuation of the war by other than military means. From this point of view the cold war is a perfectly normal state of affairs, as is also the division of world politics between two great centers of power. It follows that neutrality is literally impossible. If, for example, the non-Communist nations of Western Europe were to adopt a policy of neutrality between the United States and Russia, this would be merely an ideological illusion; it would not alter the fact that in the end they would be dominated by one side or the other. The illusion might, of course, create opportunities that would make it easier to dominate them, and a Communist assumes that the United States would exploit these opportunities as certainly, and as unscrupulously, as Russia would. Politics is a total commitment, all or nothing, a struggle with only two sides in which the deciding factor is always power. Any foreign government is either a friend or an enemy and in the last resort either totally a friend or totally an enemy. Each of the two hostile centers of power draws into its orbit the satellite states within its spheres of influence and uses them to increase its power. This is always the actual state of affairs, and talk about the rights of neutrals or of weak nations is either sentimental nonsense or hypocrisy.

When this theory of international politics is logically followed out, it changes very profoundly the meaning of several political concepts, as compared with the meaning which Americans habitually attach to them. Consider, for example, the three following terms: compromise, negotiation, alliance.

In the American political vocabulary the word "compromise" has in general a good connotation. It suggests meeting another person half way, seeing some merit in the other side, emphasizing points of agreement, agreeing to differ where differences are not vital, and in general adopting a live-and-let-live attitude. From the Russian point of view "compromise" is a bad word. It connotes lack of conviction and of principle. For in truth there is no merit in an opponent's position. Every question has only two sides, and one side is right and the other wrong. Compromise is merely a sign of weakness, an unfortunate necessity when you cannot enforce your own position, but really a kind of temporizing with evil. Margaret Mead [7] quotes the following from a report of an American negotiator who had had considerable experience in dealing with Russians: "We think of compromise as a natural way to get on with the job, but to them 'compromise' is usually coupled with the adjective 'rotten.' They are puzzled by our emphasis on the desirability of compromise."

The two valuations of compromise imply two equally different ways of regarding the aims of negotiation. An American assumes that the purpose of negotiation is to explore differences in order to reach as much agreement as the situation permits. Its object is to reduce tension, to avoid misunderstandings, and to find a basis for doing business together. From the Russian point of view negotiation is primarily a way of feeling out an opponent's position and getting a clear idea of relationships of power. Negotiation and diplomacy are more similar to espionage than they are to making a business arrangement. Stalin once said that the expression "sincere diplomacy" is as nonsensical as "dry water." To negotiate in a really conciliatory spirit would merely invite aggression, and a profession of friendship from an opponent is always to be viewed as a trap.

Finally, the meanings that Russians attach to compromise and negotiation determine the senses in which an alliance between nations is understood. In the case of nations considered to be friendly there is no important distinction between an ally and a satellite. A nation within the Communist orbit can have no valid freedom or interest against Russia. Being Communist is taken to override all other differences, and what is good for Russia is good for her allies. It is assumed that any alliance such as the European Defense Community (EDC) would be equally dominated by the United States. In the case of nations considered hostile, an alliance is merely a maneuver or a tactical expedient like a truce in war. Each side enters the agreement for its own temporary advantage and will break the agreement when its interests so direct. Any alliance between Communist and capitalist nations will be of this sort. They may "coexist" for long periods if their power is equally balanced, but sooner or later the "contradictions" between the two systems will make them enemies again.

When the class struggle is taken as its main premise Russian ideology is excessively rigid and inflexibly hostile, offering no opening at all to a policymaker whose purpose is to avoid conflict. But there is a German proverb which says, "The soup is not eaten as hot as it is cooked," and as was said above, an ideology often has two strings to its bow. There is, in fact, another side to Russian ideology and one that offers much better chances for staving off open war. This may be illustrated by the following three characteristics.

---

[7] Margaret Mead, *Soviet Attitudes Toward Authority*, N.Y., McGraw-Hill, 1951, p. 15.

First, though it is an article of faith that communism is certain to win out over capitalism and to spread to all nations, this prediction carries no time schedule with it. Communism has, so to speak, all the time there is. Ever since Marx first formulated his philosophy, before the middle of the 19th century, Marxists have tended to predict that world revolution is just around the corner. The fact that the predictions never came off is not regarded as making the final outcome any less certain. The triumph of communism can always be postponed, as Stalin postponed it when he decided that communism was possible in one country. Hence the final push to bring it into being does not have to be made at any specified time.

Second, though compromise is always, from a Communist standpoint, a dubious procedure, it is also an inevitable part of politics. In general Communist philosophy does not regard the advance toward communism as running along a straight line but rather as a zigzag. Hence its predictions are vague not only as to time but as to manner; communism will certainly triumph but no one can say exactly by what steps. From the time when Lenin switched to the New Economic Policy in 1921 the course of Russian policy both at home and abroad has included many reversals and changes of direction, when a change seemed necessary to consolidate the Party's power. Its ideology includes the belief that setbacks are to be expected and must not be taken as too discouraging. Pronouncements by the Bolshevik leadership have commonly stressed the idea that retreat is as important in successful strategy as attack. It was this, according to Stalin, that made the German military strategist Clausewitz one of Lenin's favorite authors. "Retreat under unfavorable circumstances is just as lawful a form of struggle as an offensive." The essence of sound strategy is continuous pressure, but pressure may be kept up in giving way as well as in advancing. Thus Mr. Kennan wrote in the now famous article that he published in *Foreign Affairs* in 1947: "If it [the Kremlin] finds unassailable barriers in its path, it accepts these philosophically and accommodates itself to them." [8]

Third, at least up to the present time, Bolshevik ideology has tended to deprecate anything in the nature of adventure or taking long chances. It was this which prompted Stalin's boast to Anthony Eden in 1941: "Hitler is a very able man but he does not know when to stop; I do." The pose of Bolshevik ideology is one of ultra-rationality, of constant dependence on "calculation," of being "scientific." Hence it tends to stress the dangers of political gambling, of relying on intuition or luck, or indeed of allowing feeling of any kind to influence a decision. There is at least a fair presumption that Bolshevik foreign policy would hesitate to take a course in which defeat would jeopardize

---

[8] Mr. X (George F. Kennan), "The Sources of Soviet Conduct," *Foreign Affairs*, July 1947, vol. 25, No. 4.

its position at home. In general its policy seems to be to avoid a final commitment and to keep a line of retreat open, unless it feels assured of success without meeting obstacles that are too formidable. Its maxim seems to be to press every advantage to the utmost but not to risk a major setback that would injure its long-term position.

If these appraisals of Communist ideology are correct, they imply that Bolshevik foreign policy will be rigid and dogmatic with respect to its goal but not unamenable to counterpressure steadily applied with respect to particular events and situations. And this in turn suggests some main lines of a strategy to control its expansive drive without offering it a reason to see in war an opportunity favorable to its progress. Such a policy must walk a narrow line between appeasement and provocation, because a show of friendship will be interpreted as weakness but a threat may induce the belief that good strategy lies in being the attacker. There is no reasonable doubt that an American policy which could plausibly be represented as an attack on Russia would solidify the nation behind the Bolshevik leadership, no matter how serious internal discontent with Bolshevik government may be. A policy of control calls for good nerves, because the tension will not soon be relaxed and also because loss of temper is loss of control. Within Bolshevik ideology an opponent's rage or blustering or threatening indicates that your blow has landed. The policy calls for endless patience and for limited objectives clearly conceived and persistently sought, for uncertainty or fumbling will be construed as an opportunity for penetration. It must operate on the difficult principle that ends are not negotiable and provide no ground for mutual understanding, though means can be adjusted and modified to almost any extent that does not entail too much loss of face. Negotiation has to be continuous and yet it can never be definitive. Above all a successful policy of control must have behind it a united front both at home and among the allied nations that make up the opposition to communism. For mutual distrust and recrimination, suspicion, disunity, and bickering will be interpreted as signs that the front is shaky, that it offers crevices where a lever can be inserted to pry the parties or the allies apart. On the other hand nothing is more disconcerting than a firm and voluntary alliance, not only because it can be effective but because it refutes the Communist dogma that a non-Communist society cannot be cohesive and that nations cannot cooperate if they remain free. This is one of those things which, according to Communist philosophy, cannot happen and is correspondingly disconcerting if it does happen. A policy of controlling the ideological conflict must try to make it happen, and any party or individual that makes it difficult does just that much to weaken a policy of control.

II
THE SOVIET ORGANIZATION OF THE PSYCHOLOGICAL WEAPON [1]

The need for a strong propaganda effort was recognized early by the Communists. In the *Theses and Statutes of the Third (Communist) International*, adopted by the Second Congress in 1920, the Communists called for the establishment of a periodical press, stating:

> For the struggle against [the] state of things the Communist parties must create a new type of periodical press for extensive circulation among the workmen:
>
> 1) Lawful publications, in which the Communists without calling themselves such and without mentioning their connection with the party, *learn to utilize the slightest liberty allowed by the laws*, as the Bolsheviks did at the "time of the Tsar," after 1905.
>
> 2) Illegal sheets, although of the smallest dimensions and irregularly published, but, reproduced in most of the printing offices by the workingmen (in secret, or if the movement has grown stronger, *by means of a revolutionary seizure of the printing offices*), giving the proletariat undiluted revolutionary information and the revolutionary mottoes. *Without a Communist press the preparation for the dictatorship of the proletariat is impossible.*[2]

During the growth of the Soviet state and the world Communist movement, Communist leaders stressed the importance of propaganda to Communist objectives.

Lenin, reporting to the Ninth Congress of the CPSU in March 1920, noted:

> It was only because of the Party's vigilance and its strict discipline, because the authority of the Party united all Government Departments and institutions, *because the slogans issued by the Central Committee were taken up by millions of people like one man* . . . that the miracle could take place which actually did take place. It was only because of this that we were able to win.[3]

And Stalin, in his lectures on "The Foundations of Leninism" in 1924, stated:

> It does not suffice that the vanguard should realize the impossibility of maintaining the old order and the need for its overthrow. The masses,

---

[1] The text for this chapter is taken from *Target: The World*, edited by Evron M. Kirkpatrick, © The Macmillan Company, 1957 and used with their permission.

[2] (Italics added.) *Theses and Statutes of the Third (Communist) International* (Moscow, Publishing Office of the Communist International, 1920; reprinted by the United Communist Party of America).

[3] (Italics added.) V. Yakovlev, "Lenin, Great Founder of the Soviet State," *USSR Embassy Information Bulletin,* April 28, 1950, X, 8, pp. 225, 227.

likewise, the millionfold masses, must come to understand this need. . . . *Our task is to see that the masses shall be provided with opportunities for the acquirement of such an understanding.* . . .

Communist leaders were fully aware, however, that propaganda without direction, strict discipline, and firm organization would not satisfactorily serve the purposes of the Communist movement. Lenin, setting forth "Conditions of Affiliation to the Communist International" (1920), stated:

> The periodical and nonperiodical press and *all publishing enterprises must be entirely subordinated to the Central Committee of the Party,* irrespective of whether the party as a whole is legal or illegal at the given moment; *publishing enterprises must not be permitted to abuse their autonomy by pursuing a policy that is not entirely the party policy.*[5]

AGITPROP—PROPAGANDA CONTROL BODY

An important development aimed at providing this tight control stemmed from the Eighteenth Party Congress in 1939. The Central Committee proposed a resolution toward the strengthening of Party propaganda work which stated, in part:

> . . . to concentrate the work of party propaganda and agitation in *one body* and to merge the propaganda and agitation departments and the press departments into a single Propaganda and Agitation Administration of the Central Committee of the CPSU(b).[6]

This resolution was significant because it centralized the direction of propaganda and agitation in one body. Moreover, it put this new body at the top of the Party hierarchy, directly under the Central Committee, thus firmly establishing the importance of propaganda in the Communist movement.

In this manner the present Agitprop—the section (or Department) for Agitation and Propaganda—was born. Agitprop is the central policy organization behind the propagation of the Communist doctrine throughout the world. As the resolution states, Agitprop operates directly under the Central Committee of the CPSU and is therefore one of the principal Party organs.

It is important to note the distinction made between propaganda and agitation in the resolution of the Eighteenth Party Congress cited above. This distinction was first made by George Plekhanov, founder of the first Marxist party in Russia in 1883 and Lenin's teacher. Lenin preserved the distinction, and defined the responsibilities of the propagandist and the agitator, stating:

---

[4] (Italics added.) J. Stalin, excerpt from "The Foundations of Leninism" as reprinted in *The Strategy and Tactics of World Communism* (House Document No. 619, 80th Congress, 1948), p. 107.

[5] (Italics added.) *Selected Works* (New York, International Publishers, 1943), X, 204. Statement of requirements a national Communist Party must meet before it could join the Comintern.

[6] Stalin, *op. cit.,* p. 789.

24

A propangandist dealing with, say, the question of unemployment, must explain the capitalistic nature of crises, the reasons why crises are inevitable in modern society, must describe how present society must inevitably become transformed into socialist society, etc. In a word, he must present *"many ideas."* . . . An *agitator*, however, speaking on the same subject, will take as an illustration a fact that is most widely known and outstanding among his audience, say, the death from starvation of the family of an unemployed worker, the growing impoverishment, etc., and utilizing this fact, which is known to all and sundry, will direct all his efforts to presenting a *single idea* to the "masses," i.e. the idea of the senseless contradiction between the increase in wealth and increase in poverty; he will strive to raise discontent and indignation among the masses against this crying injustice, and leave a more complete explanation of this contradiction to the propagandist. *Consequently, the propagandist operates chiefly by means of the printed word; the agitator operates with the living (spoken) word.*[7]

This distinction remains in present Communist propaganda theory and is reflected in the organization and functions of Agitprop.

PROPAGANDA COMMAND AND COMMUNICATIONS

A simplified diagram showing lines of Communist propaganda control appears in the following chart: This diagram is not intended to show "administrative" lines of control, most of which emanate from the Central Committee's Foreign Section, but rather to illustrate the lines of propaganda policy control which channel through Agitprop.

The Presidium of the Central Committee of the CPSU, the small group which rules the Communist Party and thus the Soviet Government, directs the worldwide Communist propaganda network. Charged with combining revolutionary theory and practice to give strategic and tactical direction, it is responsible for determining the tactical "line" of the Party on all major questions of current policy.

Once the "line" is determined by the Presidium of the Central Committee, Agitprop—a policy staff producing little propaganda material of its own—acts as planner, director, and "watchdog" of all Communist media engaging in propaganda dissemination. These functions are exercised both over internal and over external propaganda. For internal propaganda the flow of direction is from the CPSU Central Committee directly to Agitprop to *Pravda*, thence to internal media— the Home Service radio, *Izvestiya*, the Mosfilm Studio, and other domestic media. For external propaganda the flow of direction is from the Central Committee of the CPSU through Agitprop, coordinating with the Foreign Section to "inform" Communist diplomatic and other missions of propaganda policy and to assure necessary administrative support.

---

[7] (Italics added.) "What Is To Be Done?" (1901–1902), *Selected Works* (London, Lawrence and Wishart, Ltd., 1936), II, 85–86.

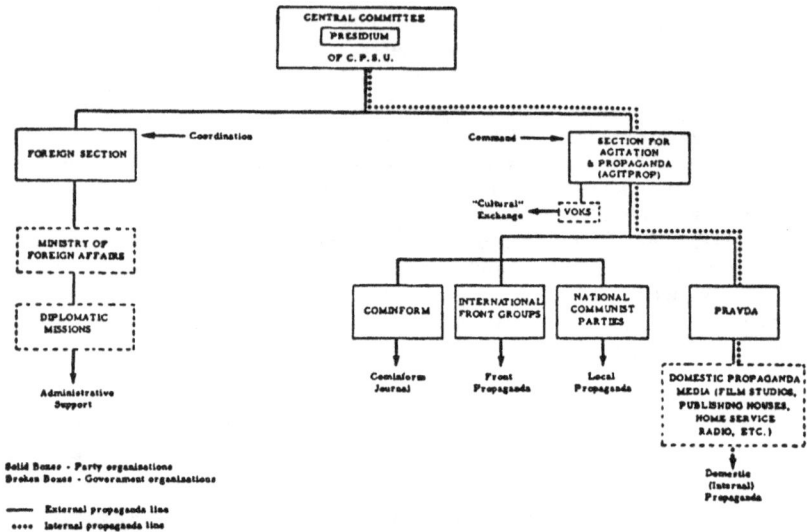

Thus, Agitprop propaganda directives become "Party line orders" spread quickly throughout the worldwide Communist network. Tight organization and the application of democratic centralism permits the semblance of "one voice"—that is, consistency of statement—for Communists everywhere speaking on any issue. This "unity of voice" is obvious to those who study Communist propaganda themes on a global basis. The control mechanism and regimentation are such that should a sudden shift in Kremlin policy occur, there is little time lost before all but the most isolated Communists conform to the new "line." Agitprop in its role of "watchdog" keeps constant check on whether the new line is being followed by the Satellites, "national" Communist parties and Communist front groups, all of which have almost identical Agitprop organizations on a smaller scale.

Propaganda guidance reaches the "national" Communist parties and front organizations in several ways. Normal methods of "guidance" and "exchange of experience" (instruction) are overt. The Cominform journal, *For a Lasting Peace, For a People's Democracy!*, published weekly in Bucharest in nearly twenty languages, disseminates the Party line through its articles. Tass transmissions often contain propaganda instructions in the form of "news items." The CPSU theatrical journal *Kommunist* interprets the Party line on a monthly basis. *Agitator's Notebooks*, published every 10 days in almost every language, interpret the Party line on timely subjects, of both domestic and international interest—usually treating one or a very few themes. *Pravda* and *Izvestiya* editorials also guide propa-

26

gandists in determining the "correct" line on current issues, and Soviet delegations to foreign nations occasionally help in transmitting Moscow directives to local Party organizations in the countries they are visiting.

Each year on May Day and on the anniversary of the Bolshevik revolution, the Party publishes a long list of *slogans*, which are action directives stemming from the CPSU Central Committee by way of Agitprop, and which are aimed at the lower echelons of Party leaders.

The means of transmission most commonly used for propaganda guidance of covert operations are couriers, the diplomatic pouch, agent radios, and coded mail.

AGITPROP ORGANIZATION

The Agitprop organization is elaborate, consisting of approximately fourteen subsections or departments, as follows:

Propaganda (administrative)	Fictional Literature
Agitation (administrative)	Art Affairs
Central (Moscow) Press	Cutural Enlightenment
Local (Provincial) Press	Schools
Publishing Houses	Science
Films (Sov Film)	Party Propaganda—Mass Agitation
Radio	VOKS

Although VOKS (the All-Union Society for Cultural Relations with Foreign Countries) assumes the posture of an autonomous— and even public—society, it is included above as a department of Agitprop because for all practical purposes it is an integral arm of the propaganda apparatus subject to Agitprop direction and control.

VOKS is responsible for all cultural exchange matters and relations with the innumerable "friendship societies" throughout the world. Organizationally, it is an administrative department divided into geographic area sections. VOKS maintains committees of prominent Soviet artists and specialists from all fields of culture who act as advisers in the selection of representatives and cultural materials (for example, films, art, and literature) which are to be sent abroad by VOKS to illustrate Soviet accomplishment. Committees are established for the natural sciences and mathematics, history, economics, theater, literature, music, architecture, sports, films, and so on.

VOKS also produces a number of newsletters and bulletins and a bimonthly magazine, the *VOKS Bulletin*, in several foreign languages.

MASS ORGANIZATIONS: FACADE FOR THE PARTY

Becoming increasingly important in the Communist propaganda apparatus are international front groups, or "mass organizations," as they are known in Communist parlance. These groups perform several vital functions for the Party. When first conceived and

27

organized (most were formed during the period of international euphoria immediately following World War II), their principal aim unquestionably was to enlist unwitting support for, and participation in, Communist causes by non-Party members who would not knowingly affiliate with the Party or with Party-sponsored organizations. However, through the years the role of mass organizations in the Communist conspiracy has expanded both in scope and in magnitude.

Because of frequent public exposure of Communist fraction control of these organizations by the Free World press and other media, their original objective of attracting persons not considered to be Party members or sympathizers has been modified to some extent. It might be safely said that the main roles of such groups today are:

1. *To produce and disseminate increasingly large quantities of printed propaganda throughout the world.* (One of the principal advantages to the Communist governments of having this function performed by the front groups is to be able to disclaim official responsibility for this activity in the face of charges of bias frequently directed at propaganda of official origin and protests by the governments of receiving countries. These disclaimers, however, are easily rebutted by the knowledge that the operating budgets for the various front groups are normally provided by the Satellite country in which the headquarters are located. Satellite governments also make available printing facilities and paper, especially the latter, which, although in critically short supply, is always available to the fronts in practically any desired quantity.)

2. *To provide "popular" support for Communist foreign policy objectives.* (Here is a modern Communist version of the "Mister Gallagher and Mister Shean" vaudeville routine. The front group passes a resolution, for example, to ban tests of atomic weapons. The USSR quickly responds to the "will of the people" and calls officially for such a ban. Or on the other hand, the USSR officially proposes a disarmament plan, and the front soon thereafter passes a similar resolution, thus providing "popular support" for the Soviet proposal.)

3. *To dupe well intentioned, but politically naïve persons into supporting party objectives.* (This task remains an important function of front groups despite the mounting difficulty of maintaining the illusion of independent action with the growing public awareness of the true nature of these organizations.)

4. *To serve as a nongovernmental channel for sponsoring free or low-cost trips to Iron and Bamboo Curtain countries.* (The recipient of such a trip explains on his return that his glowing accounts of the countries visited are unbiased because his expenses and entertainment were not paid by the governments concerned, but by a "private" international organization.)

5. *To recruit, test, and train potential Party members and functionaries.* ("Promising" members of front groups who have consistently and faithfully demonstrated their support for Party objectives often are approached to become either open or secret members of the Party. Actual Party members sometimes serve for a period in a front group either to test their loyalty and ability or to train them for higher Party responsibilities.)

ORGANIZATION OF COMMUNIST INTERNATIONAL-FRONT GROUPS

As might be expected, Communist-front groups organizationally have much in common with the Communist parties themselves. Thus the international, or geographic, organization of the various fronts coincides with that of the Party, with national, regional, district, local, and primary unit structures fanning out from the international headquarters organization. Among other obvious advantages of such a structure, it permits the ready application of "democratic centralism" both laterally, from concealed Party fractions responsible to the corresponding Party level, and vertically from the front hierarchy itself.

The internal administrative and policy organization of the international front headquarters again provides for maximum Party control. As shown on page 30, at the very apex of the organization is a "congress," followed, in descending rank but in ascending order of importance, by a council, an executive committee or bureau, and a secretariat. Finally, specialized groups known variously as bureaus, committees, or departments work under the secretariat, usually in an "advisory" capacity.

The congress nominally is in control of the group. It consists of a large number of delegates from the national groups within the front selected normally on the basis of proportional representation. This group meets briefly only about once every 2 or 3 years to hear speeches prepared and cleared in advance on an agenda previously drawn up by the bureau and secretariat. The congress thus is little more than a "rubber stamp" organization. Because most fronts now are representative only of national groups from behind the curtain, the Communists and fellow travelers greatly outnumber the other delegates and assure the passage of the Communist-prepared proposals without significant deviation.

The council is a smaller body which meets annually to go through with much the same routine. It normally is comprised of an approximately equal number of delegates from each national affiliate. Although the number of delegates from Communist countries in the council is smaller than in the congress, Communists and fellow trav-

TYPICAL FRONT STRUCTURE: WORLD FEDERATION OF DEMOCRATIC YOUTH

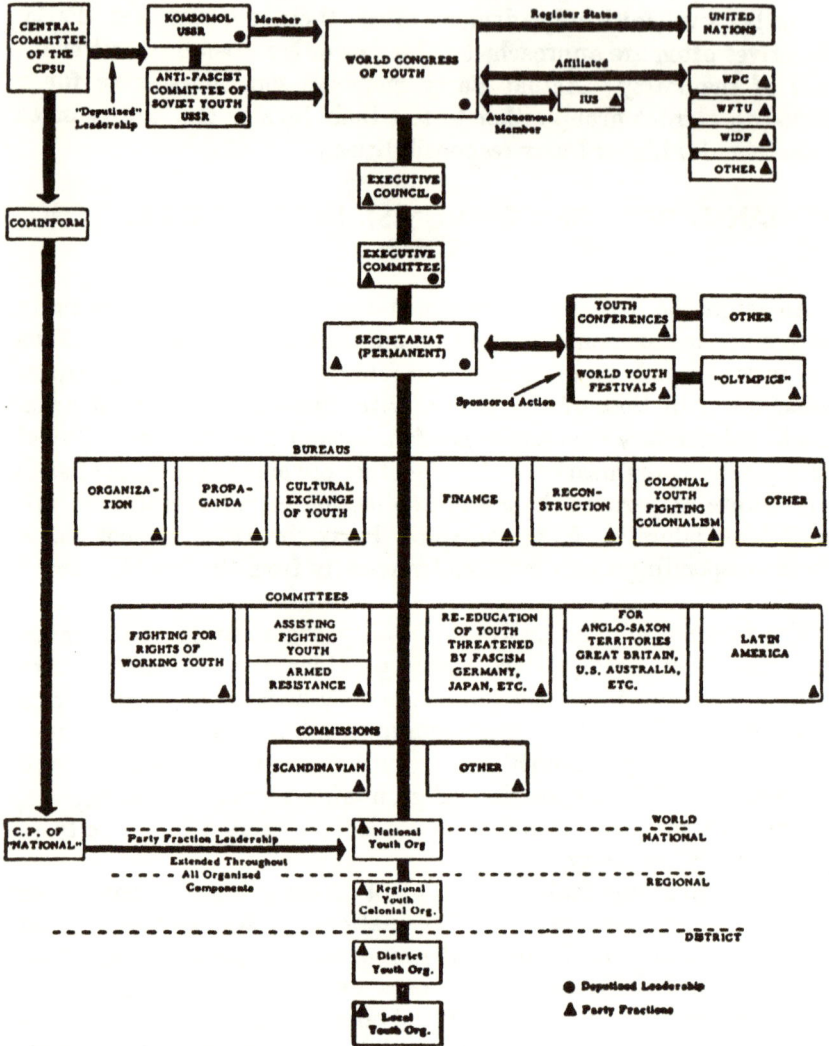

CENTRAL COMMITTEE OF THE CPSU

KOMSOMOL USSR ● — Member

ANTI-FASCIST COMMITTEE OF SOVIET YOUTH USSR ●

WORLD CONGRESS OF YOUTH ●

Register Status → UNITED NATIONS

Affiliated

IUS ▲ — Autonomous Member

WPC ▲
WFTU ▲
WIDF ▲
OTHER ▲

"Deputized" Leadership

COMINFORM

EXECUTIVE ▲ COUNCIL ●

EXECUTIVE COMMITTEE ●

SECRETARIAT (PERMANENT) ▲

YOUTH CONFERENCES ▲ — OTHER ▲

WORLD YOUTH FESTIVALS ▲ — "OLYMPICS" ▲

Sponsored Action

BUREAUS

| ORGANIZATION ▲ | PROPAGANDA ▲ | CULTURAL EXCHANGE OF YOUTH ▲ | FINANCE ▲ | RECONSTRUCTION ▲ | COLONIAL YOUTH FIGHTING COLONIALISM ▲ | OTHER ▲ |

COMMITTEES

| FIGHTING FOR RIGHTS OF WORKING YOUTH ▲ | ASSISTING FIGHTING YOUTH / ARMED RESISTANCE ▲ | RE-EDUCATION OF YOUTH THREATENED BY FASCISM GERMANY, JAPAN, ETC. ▲ | FOR ANGLO-SAXON TERRITORIES GREAT BRITAIN, U.S. AUSTRALIA, ETC. | LATIN AMERICA ▲ |

COMMISSIONS

| SCANDINAVIAN ▲ | OTHER ▲ |

C.P. OF "NATIONAL"

Party Fraction Leadership Extended Throughout All Organized Components

▲ National Youth Org. — — — WORLD NATIONAL

▲ Regional Youth Colonial Org. — REGIONAL

▲ District Youth Org. — DISTRICT

▲ Local Youth Org.

● Deputized Leadership
▲ Party Fractions

---

elers are again in the majority, because most of the national affiliates are themselves Communist fronts and appoint Communists or sympathizers to represent them.

The bureau, or executive committee, is either elected or appointed by the council, and is the principal *de facto* policymaking organ of the front. It meets several times a year and issues directives to be carried out by the permanent secretariat, appointed by the bureau.

The secretariat is the day-to-day operating and administrative arm of the front. It is almost solidly Communist, and rarely deviates from the line handed down, through various channels and cutouts, from CPSU Agitprop.

Various departments, committees, or bureaus extend outward from the secretariat level and ostensibly advise the secretariat on specialized matters, such as travel and exchange, press and information, finance, administration, organization, and so on. Actually, many of these groups are "paper" groups in evidence only on the organizational chart. However, some of them operate actively, usually as a section of the secretariat. It is here that each front group maintains, under different names, its miniature Agitprop.

Throughout the upper echelons of the front structure, there exists an "interlocking directorate" of officers and personnel from other front groups, who serve in the same or similar capacity in both groups. These people provide coordination to the activities of the various fronts and insure adherence to the overall propaganda line.

Further, in the Soviet Union and in other Communist states, model mass organizations exist which correspond to the various international fronts. These counterpart organizations, which invariably are the Communist "national" affiliates to the front groups, provide through their officers and leaders at the international level the proper Party "guidance" and "exchange of experience" to the front organization.

PRINCIPAL FRONT GROUPS

The principal front organizations are as follows:

Organization	Symbol	Headquarters
World Peace Council	WPC	Vienna.
World Federation of Trade Unions	WFTU	Prague.
International Union of Students	IUS	Prague.
World Federation of Democratic Youth	WFDY	Budapest.
Women's International Democratic Federation	WIDF	East Berlin.
International Association of Democratic Lawyers	IADL	Brussels.
World Federation of Scientific Workers	WFSW	London.
World Federation of Teachers' Unions	FISE	Vienna.
International Organization of Journalists	IOJ	Prague.
International Broadcasting Organization	OIR	Prague.
International Federation of Resistance Fighters, of Victims and Prisoners of Fascism.	FIR	Vienna.
Committee for the Promotion of International Trade	CPIT	Vienna.
World Congress of Doctors	WCD	Vienna.

Many front groups carry on their own propaganda activities—under the direction and guidance of Agitprop, CPSU—through publication programs.

A number of front groups have subsidiary organizations which also engage in the production and dissemination of propaganda material. The International Union of Students, for example, publishes magazines for agricultural students, architectural students, and medical students, and several of the trade-union internationals under the aegis of the World Federation of Trade Unions have their own periodical publications.

III
U.S. FOREIGN PSYCHOLOGICAL OPERATIONS: BACK-GROUND AND DESCRIPTION [1]

Psychological warfare, or psychological operations as many today prefer to call such activities, has been employed by agents of the United States in support of political and military operations in every war and major international crisis since 1776. However, it was not until World War I that any special organizational arrangements were made in either the military establishment or the executive branch of the Government for the conduct of such operations. The Committee On Public Information, popularly known as the "Creel Committee," and a propaganda subsection of G–2 in the American Expeditionary Force (AEF) during World War I were the first specially created agencies charged with the conduct of the Nation's foreign information program. With the end of the war both agencies went out of existence.

Prior to World War I and during the interwar period from 1919 to 1941 virtually all of the Nation's propaganda effort was conducted on an *ad hoc* basis with relatively little thought of any subsidiary or coincidental consequences of such propaganda or psychological operations. There were no agencies prior to 1938 specifically charged with any responsibilty for a U.S. propaganda effort.

During the pre-World War II buildup of the German Nazi, Italian Fascist, and Japanese Imperial war-oriented regimes the U.S. Government did little planning to counter the claims of freedom's adversaries. Prior to the late summer of 1941 the only positive governmental action taken was the creation in 1938 of an Interdepartmental Committee for Scientific and Cultural Cooperation (SCC) and a Division of Cultural Cooperation (CU) in the Department of State. These agencies were the first U.S. Government bodies to be concerned with international propaganda activities in peacetime and their interest was confined largely to the Western Hemisphere. In 1941 the Office of the Coordinator for Inter-American Affairs (CIAA) was established as a separate agency. One of its missions was to disseminate information about the United States to the peoples in Latin America.

---

[1] This chapter was prepared by William E. Daugherty, Operations Research Office, Johns Hopkins University.

U.S. PROPAGANDA ORGANIZATION IN WORLD WAR II

Beginning in the late summer of 1941 and continuing through World War II a number of government agencies were established to carry on the Nation's propaganda effort abroad. These included the Foreign Information Service (FIS), under playwright Robert E. Sherwood, in William Donovan's COI (Coordinator of Information); the Office of Facts and Figures (OFF); the Office of War Information (OWI) which was created by a merger of FIS, OFF, and other information agencies in June 1942; and the Office of Strategic Service (OSS). The radio branch of FIS (later OWI) which came to be known as the Voice of America (VOA) beamed its first shortwave broadcast overseas in March 1942. Later, at the height of the war, operating largely from New York and San Francisco, it beamed abroad more than 3,200 live programs weekly in some 40 different languages.

Within the military establishment in Washington both the War Department and the Department of the Navy established a small service group and special units and staff sections were established or improvised in most overseas commands to carry out an aggressive propaganda campaign against enemy military forces and civilians in or near the battlezone.

Late in 1944 a small office known as the Division of International Information (INI) was established in the Department of State. It coordinated its activities with those of CIAA and OWI.

At the end of World War II many government agencies were concerned with various aspects of the U.S. international information program: OWI, OSS, CIAA, CU, INI, and psychological warfare staff sections and units of the Armed Forces in Europe and the Far East.

CHANGES IN THE IMMEDIATE POSTWAR YEARS

With the end of World War II most of the government agencies concerned with international information were abolished. President Truman on 31 August 1945, by Executive Order 9608, established an Interim International Information Service (IIIS) in the Department of State and transferred to it the overseas information functions of OWI and CIAA. With this Order many of the wartime employees of these two agencies who wished to remain in government information work were transferred to IIIS. The President, by his order, authorized the Secretary of State to continue, within the Department of State for the time being, such foreign information functions as he considered necessary; to abolish any as he thought desirable; and to transfer any as he considered desirable to other executive agencies.

OWI and IIIS were both to be liquidated no later than 31 December 1945. Between 31 August and 31 December, the Secretary of State was to study the problem of foreign information and to recommend what government information program, if any, was to be conducted after 31 December 1945.

William Benton, a professional public relations counselor who was later Senator from Connecticut, was appointed Assistant Secretary of State for Public Affairs and was given administrative supervision over the foreign information program. Mr. Benton faced a formidable task in his new assignment: the winning of Congressional understanding and approval for a nonwartime international propaganda effort in order to secure funds with which to operate; the gaining of a sympathetic understanding of the requirements of the new service from both top-echelon and rank-and-file members of the Department of State and the U.S. Foreign Service; and the establishment of proper liaison procedures with responsible intelligence-collecting and policymaking officers both within and outside the Department of State.

The study of international information requirements, requested by President Truman, led to the recommendations of a committee headed by Professor Arthur MacMahon of Columbia University that there be established within the Department of State an agency to carry on the foreign information program inaugurated during the war. Accordingly in 1946, the Office of International Information and Cultural Affairs (OIC) was created and to it were transferred some of the functions of IIIS; however, operations were projected on a greatly reduced basis. All radio activities of the VOA were centralized in New York City. The number of languages in which broadcasts were to be made was reduced from 40 to 24 and the number of live shortwave programs reduced accordingly.

Congress was not enthusiastic about continuing the international information program and therefore reduced appropriations for such activities. Production of booklets and all translation programs were stopped and except for the Russian language AMERIKA the production of all wartime magazines ceased. Motion picture and press programs were continued but on a greatly reduced scale.

In 1947 further reductions in appropriations led to a reorganization of the information program. OIC was changed to the Office of International Information and Educational Exchange (OIE) in the Department of State. The activities of this office included—(a) the administration of the Fulbright Act and other educational exchange programs; (b) the establishment and supervision of U.S. Government participation in the binational institutes abroad; and (c) the administration of further reduced radio (VOA), press and motion picture programs.

When appropriations for the fiscal year 1948 were being discussed in Congress, Representative John Taber (R–N.Y.) Chairman of the House Appropriations Committee in the 80th Congress called attention to the fact that Congress was being asked to appropriate money for an agency for which there was no enabling legislation. The action of Congressman Taber in questioning the legality of the program not only led to a reduction in funds allotted to the State Department for such activities but, in addition, his action led directly to a reorganization of the office and provided the necessary impetus for the enactment of an act formally authorizing the Department of State to engage in foreign information work.

THE SMITH-MUNDT ACT

In January 1948, Congress enacted Public Law 402, sponsored by Senator Alexander Smith of New Jersey and Congressman (now Senator) Karl Mundt of South Dakota. This law, known as the Smith-Mundt Act, directed the Secretary of State "to provide for the preparation and dissemination abroad of information about the United States, its people, and its policies, through press, publications, radio, motion pictures, and other information media, and through information centers and instructors abroad."

Public Law 402 outlined the peacetime role of international information as one means of increasing "mutual understanding between the peoples of the United States and the peoples of other countries." In implementing the new law, the Department of State reorganized OIE by creating two new agencies to take its place—the Office of International Information (OII), to administer the mass media functions; and the Office of Educational Exchange (OEX), to administer the exchange of persons' program and the support of libraries and educational institutions abroad.

Both OII and OEX in 1948 were placed under the administrative supervision of the Assistant Secretary of State for Public Affairs, at the time George V. Allen, a career member of the diplomatic service. Mr. Allen later became head of the U.S. Information Agency. In 1949, in response to a recommendation of the Hoover Commission the Assistant Secretary was relieved of day-to-day operational burdens and an Office of General Manager was created to direct the International Information and Educational Exchange Program (USIE), which included both OII and OEX.

With the passage of the Smith-Mundt Act the major objective of the U.S. information program became that of promoting abroad an understanding and trust of the United States. In implementing this objective a gigantic publicity campaign was undertaken to project a "full and fair" image of the United States to counter the Soviet campaign of vilification of the United States by a distortion of its international intentions. By 1950 it became widely recognized that the publicity methods adopted to sell America to foreign audiences was not meeting with great success. The methods used to tell the "American Story" often left people bewildered and confused. As a consequence resentment, not understanding, followed.

THE CAMPAIGN OF TRUTH

In 1948 the Soviet Union attempted to isolate Berlin through imposition of a blockade, thereby forcing the West to resupply West Berlin by a gigantic airlift. In 1950 North Korea attacked the Republic of Korea. In light of these events information strategists undertook a new assessment of U.S. information goals, strategies, and methods. President Truman called for a "Campaign of Truth." With the outbreak of conflict in Korea the goals of the Soviet Union and its Communist-dominated satellites became clearer. To counter Communist efforts U.S. information objectives shifted rather sharply from that of giving a "full and fair" picture of the United States to one with more definite goals. Greater emphasis was given to the development of plans to deter further aggression; to the promotion of stability and cohesion among the nations in the non-Communist world; and to inspiring the people in these states with confidence in their capacity for meeting Communist aggression—economic, political, and military.

A system of target priorities was adopted and a specialized approach was planned for reaching various audiences abroad. In short, changes in the direction, scope, and manner of implementation of U.S. information activities were inaugurated in 1950. These modifications were designed to meet specific needs growing out of the ever-widening schism that had developed between the United States, the Soviet Union, and a number of the uncommitted nations today making up the "neutral bloc."

In fiscal year 1951 the "Campaign of Truth" led to a stepped-up overseas information program and to a congressional appropriation nearly three times that of the previous year. OII increased its staff and activities when it adopted an accelerated program designed to build in the "Free World" confidence in the intentions and capability of the United States and in themselves for resisting Communist aggression. The new program also sought to expose Communist aims in various parts of the world.

The expansion of OII's activities in 1950–1951 led to changes in the organizational structure of the U.S. information program. In January 1952 OII and OEX were consolidated under an International Information Administration (IIA). IIA while remaining a part of the Department of State was accorded a higher degree of autonomy. At its head an administrator was appointed who, unlike the General Manager of USIE, reported directly to the Secretary of State or Under Secretary of State, not to the Assistant Secretary of Public Affairs. The Assistant Secretary's role in the revised setup became largely that of serving as the channel through which the State Department transmitted foreign policy guidance to IIA. The International Information Administration was at the time of its organization also given responsibility for the information and educational exchange program in Japan which was formerly administered by the U.S. Army.

FOREIGN INFORMATION ACTIVITIES IN U.S. ARMED SERVICES

With the capitulation of Germany and Japan in 1945 and the occupation of their territories, U.S. military authorities assumed responsibility for two major functions in the field of foreign information—(a) the political reorientation of former enemy people by controlling or supervising the uses for which the media of mass communications were employed in their territories; and (b) the dissemination in these areas of information, news, and propaganda originating from the United States or friendly allied sources.

The control of information and channels of mass media was historically, if not logically, an outgrowth of wartime combat psychological warfare operations in Europe, and, to a lesser extent, in Japan. In former Nazi areas the supervision over the mass media channels of communications was entrusted to an Information Control Division (ICD) of American military government in Germany when Supreme Headquarters Allied Expeditionary Forces (SHAEF) and its Psychological Warfare Division were dissolved. Much of ICD's work stemmed directly from work undertaken earlier by PWD/SHAEF. The information control program provided that—(a) the Nazi propaganda organization was to be disbanded; (b) there was to be a guided reconstruction of German information services; and (c) there was to be an Allied program designed to foster desired attitudes and ideas among the German people. These objectives were sought through censorship of German media of mass communications, by a reorganization of German information activities, by the elimination of all known Nazi sympathizers, and through a positive Allied information and propaganda program. The U.S. Army, as the occupying force in Germany, was mainly responsible for the implementation of this program. As specific objectives were achieved the machinery provided for their accomplishment was phased out. At the close of the military phase of the German occupation such information functions as remained with the occupying power were transferred to the High Commissioner's Office. Among the most significant achievements of the U.S. armed services in Germany was the establishment and management of RIAS, "Radio in the American Sector" in Berlin. RIAS is still in existence over 15 years after its establishment. It is now an integral part of the U.S. foreign information setup. Its broadcasts in German reach nearly all parts of East Germany and a number of "eavesdroppers" in borderlands are known to be fairly regular listeners.

The nature of the information control that was established in Japan differed from that instituted in Germany. In the first place, the United States was not as blessed in numbers of American propaganda specialists with wartime psychological warfare experience in the Pacific theater. Compared to Americans who knew German and Germany, few knew Japanese and Japan intimately. In the second place, in Japan, unlike postwar Germany, a Japanese government functioning after a fashion was in existence when United States troops landed. Thus it was possible for U.S. personnel to issue orders to the existing government for implementation rather than have to take direct action to accomplish desired results. The Civil Information and Education Section (CI&E) of the Supreme Commander Allied Powers (SCAP), which operated from 1945 to the end of the occupation in 1952, thus could operate with far fewer personnel than ICD in Germany. CI&E placed its major emphasis on breaking up the close connections then existing between the Japanese government and the various media of mass communication. In addition to its supervisory or control functions, CI&E undertook a number of propaganda campaigns in support of specific objectives of the operation.

Within the military establishment in Washington, staff planning functions for the use of psychological warfare in the event of war virtually ceased after 1945. In 1949 in the Department of the Army only two relatively junior officers in the Subsidiary Plans Branch of the Operations Division devoted only a part of their time to psychological warfare planning. Planning in the Navy was on an equally low level at the time whereas within the Air Force, only recently raised to a level of a separate department, one or two officers and at least three civilians were involved in psychological warfare planning.

Several months after the outbreak of conflict in Korea the Army General Staff created a special staff division—the Office of the Chief of Psychological Warfare—to supervise planning and to provide advice to military planners. Late in 1950 and early 1951 a number of reserve officers and men with propaganda qualifications were recalled to active duty. A training course was established at Fort Riley, Kans., a Loudspeaker and Leaflet (L&L) Company was activated within the Eighth Army in Korea, and two reserve Radio Broadcasting and Leaflet (RB&L) Groups (later redesignated battalions) were activated. One of the RB&L Groups was dispatched to the Far East

Command in Tokyo, the other to the headquarters of the U.S. theater command in Europe. A second L&L company was activated and dispatched to Seventh Army in Germany.

For a period of approximately 5 years, from 1950 to 1955, the growth of interest in and size of the planning staff in headquarters, and supporting units for psychological warfare in the Air Force nearly matched that of the Army, even though at no time was the Air Force given a mission corresponding to that assigned to Army units in Korea or Europe.

Planning for the employment of psychological warfare in connection with U.S. Naval operations at no time since the end of World War II has involved more than the part-time services of one or two officers.

Since the end of the Korean conflict only the Army, among the three military services, has retained a major interest in preparing propaganda personnel for use in connection with military operations in the event of a resumption of armed conflict. Unlike the situation which prevailed on 25 June 1950, the U.S. Army today enjoys a much higher state of readiness in the field of psychological warfare.

The Office of the Chief of Psychological Warfare, as a special staff section of the U.S. Army, was renamed the Office of the Chief of Special Warfare in 1957, and in 1959 the separate office was abolished and the activities transferred to the Deputy Chief of Staff for Military Operations (DCS/OPS). In June 1961 psychological warfare planning in the headquarters U.S. Army was entrusted to a small group of officers making up the Psychological Operations Branch of the Special Warfare Division in the Strategic Plans and Policy Section of DCS/OPS. The location of a small but active planning staff unit on the General Staff level in Army headquarters, the school at Fort Bragg, North Carolina, and the number and variety of active duty and reserve units in existence (some of which are deployed overseas) represent a vast improvement over the situation existing on 25 June 1950 when the North Korean Communists launched their attack on South Korea.

THE UNITED STATES INFORMATION PROGRAM STUDIED

During the 1952 presidential campaign General Dwight D. Eisenhower, as the candidate of the Republican Party, attacked the containment policy of the Truman Administration and pledged a "roll-back" of Communist influence. In a speech delivered 8 October 1952 General Eisenhower implied that if elected he would make greater use of "every means known to transmit ideas" as a means of winning other people to the cause of freedom.

Early in his new administration President Eisenhower appointed C. D. Jackson as his personal adviser on psychological warfare, and a Committee on Foreign Information Activities, headed by William

H. Jackson. Mr. C. D. Jackson, in addition to his advisory role at the White House, was also a member of the William H. Jackson Committee. The Committee recommended that all overseas information activities be consolidated in one agency within the Department of State. At the same time another committee—the President's Advisory Committee on Government Organization, headed by Nelson Rockefeller—recommended the establishment of an independent agency to implement the nation's foreign information program. The Jackson Committée accepted this proposal and it was thereupon promptly approved by the Secretary of State and Congress.

The U.S. Advisory Commission on Information, headed by Dr. Mark A. May of Yale University, after a parallel study of the overseas information program reached a similar conclusion. A subcommittee on Overseas Information Programs of the Senate Foreign Relations Committee, first led by Senator J. William Fulbright and later by Senator Bourke B. Hickenlooper, also investigated the program. The Hickenlooper Subcommittee concluded that the administrator of the information program should be given greater responsibility and authority and that, should the overseas information operations be established as an independent agency, the educational exchange program should remain a responsibility of the Department of State.

THE UNITED STATES INFORMATION AGENCY ESTABLISHED—1953

On 1 August 1953, President Eisenhower by Reorganization Plan No. 8 established the United States Information Agency (USIA). The Agency was assigned the overseas information activities of IIA, the Mutual Security Agency (MSA), and the information programs in Germany and Austria, previously administered by the Department of the Army. Reorganization Plan 8 specified that the new agency would receive foreign policy guidance from the Department of State. The Exchange of Person's Program remained in the State Department, but for operational convenience it was agreed that the USIA would administer the program overseas.

The new agency began its operation as a separate agency with reduced funds for a foreign information program and with a Congressional directive to move the VOA radio operations from New York to Washington, D.C. This move was completed in the autumn of 1954.

Theodore C. Streibert, a radio executive, was chosen as the first Director and served until November 1956 when he was succeeded by Arthur Larson, an educator, public servant, and lawyer. Mr. Larson remained only 1 year. He was succeeded by George V. Allen, previously an Assistant Secretary of State for Public Affairs. Edward R. Murrow, a noted radio and television news commentator and executive, was appointed as Director of USIA in January 1961.

The history of USIA under its first three directors is largely an account of gradually expanding operations. During the first 9 years of its existence appropriations were increased each of 5 years over that of the immediately preceding year. Its most serious appropriations' setback occurred in fiscal year 1958 when its budget request was cut by more than $20 million largely as a political move by the majority party in Congress to repudiate the then director. In the 8 years ending with fiscal year 1961 USIA has received appropriations in excess of $767 million.

At the beginning of 1961 USIA was operating at 182 posts in 89 countries abroad. Over 1,000 Americans and more than 7,000 local residents were employed in its operations overseas. The radio branch, or VOA as it is popularly called, was broadcasting short, medium, and long wave in English and 36 other languages. Transmitters were on the air daily with nearly 45 hours of original transmissions and nearly as much more as repeats of earlier broadcasts. To project the Nation's radio voice abroad USIA employed 30 transmitters located at seven separate locations in the United States. Broadcasts from these transmitters were picked up and relayed by 2 transmitters in Hawaii, 53 on foreign soil and 3 located on a floating courier ship stationed in the area of the Aegean Sea.

Media Employed. The USIA employs all media of modern communications. In addition to radio broadcasts that emanate from the United States daily, a newsfile of the latest news development and editorial comment is sent to U.S. public affairs officers stationed around the world. The newsfile upon receipt abroad is translated into the local language and made available to local news media. Motion pictures, film strips, television programs, exhibits, specialized magazines published on a fairly regular basis, pamphlets, and translations of relevant American and Free World books are a few of the channels employed by USIA in its work abroad.

At the end of 1960 USIA was supporting in whole or in part the operations of 123 binational centers in 35 countries. Among the activities sponsored by such centers was the teaching of English and the sponsoring of concerts and seminars, the showing of motion pictures, and exhibits of art objects, teaching materials, and evidences of scientific advances in the United States. All of these are designed to promote better understanding of the United States and its people.

Books about the United States were circulating at the end of 1960 from USIA libraries abroad at the rate of eight million a year. These were read largely by teachers, students, government officials, professional men and women, and other community leaders. There were in existence 164 information libraries and 91 reading rooms located in 70 Free World countries. To further promote the reading of American books USIA provides direct assistance to foreign publishers in producing translated editions of selected books.

The utilization of television outlets abroad for the dissemination of information concerning the United States has become increasingly significant in recent years. As early as 1955 USIA was sending television material weekly to 100 overseas stations most of which was used regularly by the stations. USIA technicians advised a number of foreign groups in the development of local television stations abroad. By the end of 1959 there were an estimated 32.2 million television sets in 55 countries, not including the United States and Canada. This number represented an increase of nearly 10 million over those in existence in 1958.

So important had television abroad become that USIA in November 1958 established a separate service to provide special events coverage and television features on American life. By the end of 1960 this service was being provided to stations in 51 countries, including stations in at least one country behind the Iron Curtain, Poland, where a breakthrough was accomplished in December 1959. USIA's program on Squaw Valley, Calif., the scene of the 1960 Winter Olympics, was seen on a Polish sportscast on 6 December 1959. This showing led to requests from Warsaw for other USIA television programs including ones on American Literature and automation in the United States.

ORGANIZATION OF USIA

The organization of USIA has not changed greatly since its establishment in 1953. As an independent agency of the executive branch of the Government it is responsible through the National Security Council to the President. The following illustration shows the relationship of the agency to other agencies and the departments of the executive branch.

The Department of State provides foreign policy guidance, to which the USIA conforms in the development of information programs, and it appraises and evaluates the Agency's program to assure conformity to established foreign policy. Overseas the chiefs of U.S. diplomatic missions exercise general direction and leadership over all U.S. programs, including those dealing with information, in the country of assignment. The Public Affairs Officer at U.S. embassies and legations abroad serve as the Ambassador's or Minister's local adviser on matters of public relations.

December 1960

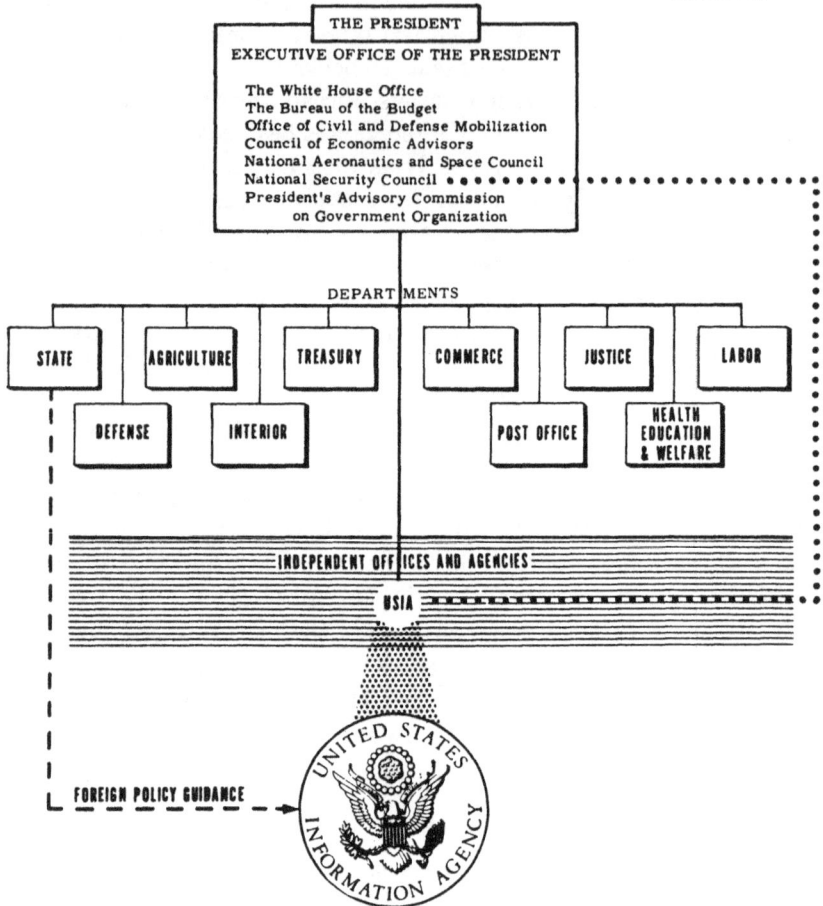

The internal organization of USIA is shown in the accompanying illustration. The Agency's tasks reflect the need for an organization that places emphasis on the fulfillment of certain staff support—administration, intelligence, and research—and in addition, on communications techniques employed and the differing needs of individual countries. Thus the Agency consists of a number of functional and geographic offices, each reporting to the Director. This illustration does not show echelons or levels of responsibility but is merely a graphic means of presenting a complex and highly integrated organization. While the figure is able to show vertical lines of responsibility it does not show the lateral, informal lines of cooperation that are necessary for the accomplishment of the Agency's mission.

DECEMBER 1960

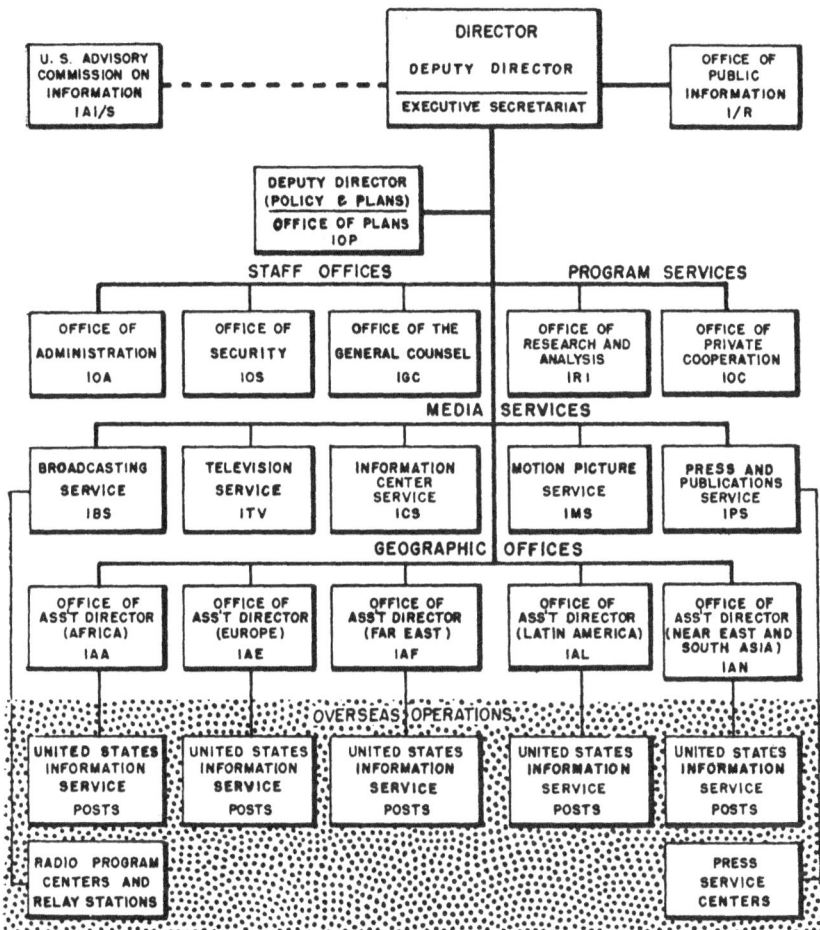

| DIRECTOR |
| DEPUTY DIRECTOR |
| EXECUTIVE SECRETARIAT |

| U. S. ADVISORY COMMISSION ON INFORMATION IAI/S | OFFICE OF PUBLIC INFORMATION I/R |

DEPUTY DIRECTOR (POLICY & PLANS) OFFICE OF PLANS IOP

STAFF OFFICES   **PROGRAM SERVICES**

| OFFICE OF ADMINISTRATION IOA | OFFICE OF SECURITY IOS | OFFICE OF THE GENERAL COUNSEL IGC | OFFICE OF RESEARCH AND ANALYSIS IRI | OFFICE OF PRIVATE COOPERATION IOC |

MEDIA SERVICES

| BROADCASTING SERVICE IBS | TELEVISION SERVICE ITV | INFORMATION CENTER SERVICE ICS | MOTION PICTURE SERVICE IMS | PRESS AND PUBLICATIONS SERVICE IPS |

GEOGRAPHIC OFFICES

| OFFICE OF ASS'T DIRECTOR (AFRICA) IAA | OFFICE OF ASS'T DIRECTOR (EUROPE) IAE | OFFICE OF ASS'T DIRECTOR (FAR EAST) IAF | OFFICE OF ASS'T DIRECTOR (LATIN AMERICA) IAL | OFFICE OF ASS'T DIRECTOR (NEAR EAST AND SOUTH ASIA) IAN |

OVERSEAS OPERATIONS

| UNITED STATES INFORMATION SERVICE POSTS | UNITED STATES INFORMATION SERVICE POSTS | UNITED STATES INFORMATION SERVICE POSTS | UNITED STATES INFORMATION SERVICE POSTS | UNITED STATES INFORMATION SERVICE POSTS |

| RADIO PROGRAM CENTERS AND RELAY STATIONS | | | | PRESS SERVICE CENTERS |

RELATIONSHIP OF USIA TO OTHER AGENCIES OF GOVERNMENT

The Director of USIA has many contacts with officials of the executive branch. Until its abolition early in 1961 he was an active member of the interdepartmental Operations Coordinating Board (OCB) and he attends meetings of the National Security Council (NSC) as an observer and he participates in its deliberations on invitation of the presiding officer, the President. He also attends meetings of the Cabinet when matters of concern to the Agency are discussed.

The Director or Deputy Director attends the daily staff meetings of the Secretary of State. Through appropriate officials, liaison is maintained with the Assistant Secretary of Defense for Public Affairs. The principal field of overlapping current interest between the Department of Defense and USIA lies in the area now described as "Cold War Planning Activity." This activity covers a wide range of functions involving public statements on military matters, overseas troop-community relations and the role of the military in peacetime psychological activities directed at foreign audiences. USIA also maintains direct liaison with the Central Intelligence Agency (CIA) through established channels at the level of the Director and the Planning Director.

Relations with the Congress are maintained through the Senate Foreign Relations Committee, the House Foreign Affairs Committee, the House and Senate Government Operations Committees, and the Senate and House Appropriations Committees. The Director, Deputy Director, and General Counsel all deal directly with individual members of the Congress on matters of Agency concern. The General Counsel is responsible for maintaining day-to-day contacts with all members of Congress and all Congressional Committees concerned with the work of the Agency.

The Agency also has three public advisory groups which advise the Director: U.S. Advisory Commission on Information, Broadcast Advisory Commission, and Advisory Commission on Cultural Information. The Agency maintains a small secretariat for all three advisory groups, headed by a full-time staff director. The Advisory Commission on Information submits periodic reports directly to Congress giving its evaluation of the Agency and recommending improvements in the program.

A SUMMARY: IN RETROSPECT AND A LOOK TO THE FUTURE

The preceding discussion of the historical development of the present day U.S. international information programs suggests the dynamic character of the activity. Most observers and assessors of past action agree as to the proper objectives, but there has not always been agreement on methods and techniques for the attainment of declared objectives. The United States has had to move more slowly than some desired for it was often necessary to learn by doing. Such being the situation, there have been frequent reorganizations of the information setup. Only slowly was the lesson brought home that the keys to successful information operations are policy and personnel. Without a U.S. policy that is attractive to foreign audiences it is difficult to influence people. Personnel with creative imagination, patience, and the ability to reach the minds of those they would persuade are equally necessary, yet such has never been available in the numbers required. To the extent that inadequately motivated and trained personnel were sent abroad to sell America its information program has suffered.

On 2 December 1959 President Eisenhower appointed a Committee on Information Activities Abroad to undertake a comprehensive survey of "The United States Information System." The Committee, headed by Mansfield D. Sprague, reported to the President on 23 December 1960. It reached three general conclusions:

a. On the whole, the U.S. information system and efforts to integrate psychological factors into policy have become increasingly effective;

b. The evolution of world affairs, the effectiveness of Communist apparatus, and the growing role of public opinion internationally confronts the United States with the necessity of continuing improvement in this aspect of government, on an orderly but urgent basis;

c. The need for an intensified information program requires the allocation of substantially greater resources during the next decade, better training of personnel, further clarification of the role of information activities, increasing the understanding and competence of government officials to deal with information and psychological matters, and improvement in the mechanics of coordination.

After his election as President, John F. Kennedy appointed a task force committee composed of Lloyd Free, Princeton University professor and one-time public affairs officer in Rome, and W. Phillips Davison, Rand Corporation, to study the requirements for an international information program. While the conclusions and recommendations of this task force group have not been formally released it is understood they are not in conflict with those offered by the Sprague Committee.

Judged by the history of the recent past and the known conclusions of recent task force study groups, one can anticipate a slow but steady growth in the size and scope of the Nation's information program during the next decade.[2] The degree to which its effectiveness will be increased will depend on two factors: the adoption of attractive policies by policymakers, and the selection and training of personnel who possess proper aptitudes and skills for the tasks assigned. Poorly trained personnel may be able to appear effective in presenting an attractive policy whereas the most skillful propagandist will have grave difficulty in selling an unattractive policy.

---

[2] One approach to international activities is the Peace Corps which was started on 1 March 1961 when President Kennedy issued an Executive order establishing the Corps on a temporary basis. It represents an opportunity for individual citizens to work directly with the people of other countries to provide economic, social, or educational assistance and to further the cause of peace through personal relationships and the development of mutual understanding. It is established as an independent agency within the Department of State. The ultimate scope and magnitude of the permanent Peace Corps will be determined by Congress.

IV

THE SOVIET PSYCHOLOGICAL APPROACH [1]

There are many disquieting indications that the Communists may have developed, or stumbled upon, an all-inclusive or a totalitarian doctrine of psychological warfare.

Perhaps the most striking characteristic of Communist propaganda is how dull and unconvincing it is. Its arguments are not logically persuasive, and their presentation is commonly repellent and unattractive. Nevertheless, communism has been able to achieve considerable successes, even in the intellectual domain.

This anomaly may have explanation in the circumstance that the Communists do not at all aim to persuade the mind. Instead they seem to be orienting the *souls* of their audience.

If we accept this as our first hypothesis, we should assume next that the techniques of soul surgery should become clearest in situations where they are easiest to apply. Hence, instead of looking for such techniques in the field of international diplomacy, we should expect that Communist psychological-warfare techniques are revealed most dramatically in the indoctrination of party members and in the activities commonly called "brainwashing" or "brain changing." The treatment of war and political prisoners, including party members, of young party recruits, and of captive populations may give more valuable hints about the Communists' secret doctrine of psychological warfare than their purely verbal efforts in so-called propaganda campaigns.

THE CONDITIONED REFLEX

The Communists have acknowledged that they owe a considerable debt to Ivan P. Pavlov and his discovery of the conditioned reflex. This theory, especially if reinterpreted, can be evolved as a supplement to the basic theorem of Marx, that a change in social conditions will transform men. In addition to rejecting the "subjective," or "will," factor, the Pavlovian or post-Pavlovian theory asserts that man's reflexes and behavior are controlled by signals—social conditions, words, and mass communication—which in turn are controllable by scientific procedures. Thus, man's behavior is decided by "objective" factors and, to the extent that those factors can be manipulated, is

---

[1] The material in this chapter was taken from Stefan T. Possony, "Communist Psychological Warfare," an article published in the *SRI Journal*, Fourth Quarter, 1959. Used by permission of the copyright owners.

determinable. The person is "other-directed" by state or party or, in their absence, by "economic forces"; therefore psychological processes can be managed, fixed, or altered; and man can be "transformed."

Fundamentally, Communists hold that behavior, especially the behavior of groups, classes, and nations, can be manipulated through the conditioning of reflexes. To a large extent this theory underlies Soviet propaganda, especially its insistence on monotonous repetition and its capture of symbolic words which, so to speak, "ring a bell." (As usual in the case of "planners," it is not specified how the planners are planned, or how the human "conditioners" can be conditioned. It can be deduced from this omission that Communists assume their own elite's freedom from the conditioned reflex mechanism.)

The Communists have learned a great deal about the interrelationships between physiology and psychology. This knowledge allows them, in their domestic and intraparty operations, to influence behavior through proper regulation of work, food, and leisure. In other words, they approach the mind through the body. The Communists appear to be consciously employing methods for inducing psychological disturbances in living organisms. By deliberate manipulation of stimuli, the desire for independent action, or the "freedom urge," is weakened or extinguished and neurotic behavior induced.

The artificial creation of insanity—a device which the Communists have applied to their prisoners by subjecting them to various forms of "invisible torture" such as uncertainty, fear, sleeplessness, strong light effects, and kneeling or standing—may not lend itself to the treatment of large numbers of people. However, unpredictable behavior, the acceleration and calming of disturbances and crises, alternations between smiles and growls, i.e., variable creations and releases of fear, and the maintenance of tension in perpetuity may induce quasi-neurotic behavior, increase the values of the "signal," and facilitate the acceptance of new word-signals. By interfering with family life and placing major emphasis on public education of infants, the father image is vested in an external and nonhuman entity, the state, or the party. This method of rearing children probably induces them to become more submissive to higher authority; it undoubtedly aims at restricting the sphere of private life and conceivably alters the emotional structure.

The Soviets make sure that the human herd obeys the "signals" of authority, while individual consciousness, emotionality, and initiative remain underdeveloped. Relegation of sex and other types of affection to minor and regressive roles is expected to induce "sublimation" through productive work and party chores. This particular technique is employed to transform human beings into mere cogs within a gigantic machine.

The Communists adopted, although not for curative purposes, the basic techniques of psychoanalysis, in particular the psychoanalytic interview. The psychoanalytic interview between physician and patient obviously would be impractical if patients were to be treated in large numbers. Hence the Communists have developed more streamlined methods that allow the mass production, not of cures, but of "complexes" and "traumas." These techniques include the compulsory writing of diaries, autobiographies, and histories of one's thought development; of oral interviews with party members; of hearings before organizational and ideological commissions and the political police; and of public "confessions."

These interviews, frequently repeated, inculcate in the "patient" feelings of error, guilt, shame, and fear, as well as desires for repentance and revenge—and provide the party with powerful levers of blackmail. This process aims to weaken the patient's conscience, to increase his will to obey and believe, stimulate his survival instincts, and augment his pliability for party purposes.

Whenever the Communists succeed in convincing people that they are a sort of incarnation of humanity's social conscience and that they are history's anointed arbiters of any action undertaken by non-Communists, a person will tend to be apologetic about any doubts he harbors concerning communism. Opposition to or deviation from communism is tantamount to a negation of mankind's loftiest ideals and of mankind's inevitable future.

The Communists try to exploit, negatively and positively, a person's relationship to communities such as his family. In this connection they have adopted or reinvented, in their own fashion, the inferiority complex and the power urge. They evoke in the "patient" various feelings of insufficiency, thus hoping to stimulate him into compensatory action that would satisfy his power cravings and those of the party.

While the therapist seeks to eliminate the sources of trouble, the Communist psychological manipulator works toward the destruction of the self-reliant personality. To employ modern terms, he tries his hand at "brainwashing." Once this operation has been completed, a supplementary activity, "brain changing," must be undertaken. The brain is emptied of mundane thoughts, while simultaneously and wherever possible the body is weakened and the sensuous drives are subdued by fatigue, hunger, deprivation, and anguish. The mind enters a state of receptivity and exaltation. At this point, thoughts, ideas, symbols, and emotions—in short, "visions"—are put into the cleansed mind. The "patient"—who may be a member of a Western Communist party or a student at a party "university"—is invited to learn by rote some of the basic texts of the Communist literature. He is asked to write down the various thoughts he considers right, and to apply the doctrine to current and concrete issues. He may even be asked to participate in conspiratorial activities and to commit himself through acts of immorality, which may range all of the way from informing and spying to the betrayal of one's parents, from leading a lynching party to straight murder. The propositions of the doctrine must be *attached to the person* by extreme emotions. Wherever possible, this process is eased by public discussions, such as "democratic criticism," confession, trials, etc., which may induce trance or, conversely, "hardening" of the soul.

The Communists extensively employ hypnotic and suggestive techniques. The student is urged to tell himself, often by mechanical repetition, that he is becoming a better Communist, that he is cutting himself loose from all the black shadows of the past, and that he desires to sacrifice himself to the cause. The "patients" themselves, while learning and acquiring the proper reflexes, must also produce the signals to which they themselves and others must react. The insistence on parrotlike repetition is designed to harden the conditioned reflexes, to maintain a system of mutual suggestion or hypnosis, and to "fix" the desired complexes.

A nation is more likely to win in conflict if it considers its cause to be just. While the attempt by a nation's leaders, during a conflict, to endow their cause with righteousness is not new, the Communists push this to the limit. The purpose is to inculcate into the Free World guilt feelings about resistance to communism and at the same time immunize the "Soviet peoples" with a sort of ideological vaccination against any notion that Communist wars or even aggressions may be something less than emanations of an exalted sense of justice. The Free World has been infected to some degree by bad conscience and guilt feelings. Hence, partly at least, the often surprising paralysis of democratic will.

The social universe is broken down into such opposing relationships as classes and strata, exploiter and exploited, class-conscious Communists and backward elements, "comrade" and enemy, organizations and inert forces, etc. The craving for justice is monopolized in the sense that, according to the suggestion, only the Communists ever can really satisfy it. Communism, to put it differently, is both a myth that fulfills the eternal human requirement for myths, and a myth that satisfies the concrete needs of orientation—it gives direction and purpose to a man's daily chores.

COMMUNIST SURROGATES FOR RELIGION

The Communist drive against religion assumes particular importance. In their attempts to undermine hostile societies, the Communists make every effort to destroy religious, ethical, and other higher motivations. They hope, thereby, that the preoccupation with immediate, mundane, material and private interests and the destruction of spiritual reserves will create frustrations and "atomize" society.

As religious beliefs wane, the number of possible recruits for communism tends to increase. This is so not only because there is a mechanical relationship between communism and atheism, but, also, more significantly, because the human hunger for redemption and assurance must be stilled and because the ingrained desire for a god craves satisfaction. Communism redeems on earth and proclaims man to be "god." The revolution is seen as the crucial "religious" event that transforms man from the object into the subject of history, i.e., into the creator of the perfect society.

The Communists' most powerful weapon in their onslaught on religion is social criticism addressed to situations of economic hardship, oppression, racial tension, delinquency, family trouble, and to shortcomings of religious organizations. The purpose of social criticism is to produce frustration-consciousness and persuade people that they cannot take such frustrations in their stride, let alone sublimate them by religious abnegation and hope for a hereafter. Instead they must overcome them by revolutionary and violent action, and by active sacrifice. Frustration, let us note, is a forerunner of aggressiveness, especially if aggressive impulses can be stimulated artificially.

The Communists must find for the societies under their rule a substitute for religion as a foundation of mental health. They cannot adopt religion, certainly not openly, because this would sensitize human conscience and thus undermine the foundations of their state and their world movement. Neither can they condone hedonistic tendencies nor any objective, probabilistic, openminded and multivalued thinking that would jeopardize their dogmatic ideology and, most significantly in our context, preclude the effective application of psychological warfare, Communist style. Their obvious solution is, first, to peddle the pseudo-religion of materialistic communism; second, to retain the aspects of religions—faith, brotherhood, initiation, salvation, redemption, grace, paradise, consecration, guilt, sin, sacrifice, atonement, asceticism—all of which have their counterparts in the Communist ideology; and third, to be excessively dogmatic about it all.

Communist dogmatism knows of saints and devils, incantations, indices of forbidden books, self-chastisement, anathemas upon heretics, ritualism, exegesis, apologetics, mysticism, and Talmudism (but not of a wailing wall for the leaders in power). This quasi-religiousness is at the bottom of the various psychoanalytic and hypnotic techniques which, without this "spiritual" foundation, probably would not "take."

There is still another way of looking at this. To the extent that communism embraces a materialistic or atheistic cosmogony, it is religion. It answers one of the basic human questions by pointing to matter, the laws of nature, and accident as the causes and meaning of the universe and, by implication, to true death and extinction as the future. Communism admits the existence of a higher power, but it assumes that power—or force—to be blind and nonpersonal. Thus, it purges religion of the concept of a higher power which is purposive, and it rejects the notion of a higher power that has revealed its purposes in terms understandable by humans. It accepts the idea that higher forces are intervening in human lives, but it assumes this intervention to be entirely accidental and meaningless. Thus, it postulates that "science" may give man a capability to influence the higher forces, nay, to dominate them, but it rejects any idea of a personal relationship of man with God.

The dictator becomes god, the only god for that matter; and the party becomes the church. As a variant, collective leadership becomes a sort of Trinity. The central committee and the local leaders take care of polytheistic needs. The parallels could be pressed further. The point is that all the essential elements of religion except the Virgin Mother complex are represented.

COMMUNIST SOCIOLOGICAL ASSUMPTIONS

Fear is frequently a cause of human difficulty; it diminishes survival capabilities of all kinds; and it is the disintegrating factor *par excellence*. This, of course, is not a new discovery. It is not surprising that the Communists always have laid great stress on terror, violence, and purges, and nowadays have enlisted the specter of nuclear war in their strategy of terror. They usually obtain good results from military threats and movements, and from giving the impression that they are willing to go beyond the "brink of war." The "specter" of communism now is in the nature of a ghost in the closet. The specter that really haunts the world is that of a technological monster heavily armed with nuclei and bacilli and propelled by jets and rockets.

However, the Communists have added an improvement to the age-old art of inducing fright. Once a phenomenon is understood and its behavior has become predictable, men no longer fear it. A danger that is perceived clearly may become a stimulant for action—a most unwelcome possibility. Consequently, the Communists have adopted the techniques of erecting impenetrable "curtains" and of acting unpredictably and capriciously. They alternate smiles with growls, arrest the innocent and free the guilty, keep prisoners in captivity beyond their terms but release them at any odd moment. In general, they show themselves impervious to reasonable argument and immovable by counsels of moderation. Deliberately, the impression is being created that one never can know what is going to happen next; even if everything is calm now, the next disturbance may be of unparalleled violence.

"Frequency modulation" in diplomacy is designed to dislocate a nation's fortitude. The technique is patterned after Hitler's pioneering attempts during 1936–1939. The ups and downs from expectations of "peace in our generation" to fears of total war, and the frequent rearrangements between business as usual and war preparedness made rational decision-making quite impossible. Although in 1939 the decision was finally made for resistance, the Communists apparently expect that in the future the democratic decision will be against nuclear war. The peace-above-all theme, punctuated and made convincing by war scares, is designed to kill the national conscience.

COMMUNIST CROWD PSYCHOLOGY

The Communists have discovered that crowds are not formed just by direct physical contacts among a mass of people, such as in meetings or demonstrations. Instead, crowd attitudes can be created among people who are physically isolated. It is merely necessary to arouse excessive fears, exploit a calamity, stimulate a panicky attitude, give signals for action against scapegoats or for actions with a symbolic character, and keep the majority of the population paralyzed. One of the great objectives is to induce in all hostile groups the attitude of no-will.

COMMUNIST SELECTION PROCESS

The Communist techniques are particularly apparent in the selection of their party members. The process embodies essentially five aspects.

1. The candidate is requested to prepare extensively biographical accounts of himself and to repeat this literary effort several times for the purpose of revealing whatever personal weaknesses or strengths he might have.

2. The individual must show a capability of absorbing the Communist doctrine and at the same time eliminating non-Communist thoughts. This result is achieved by restricting his reading to approved Communist texts, by having him learn many of these by rote, and by keeping track, through diaries, of the person's intellectual development.

3. In accepting an individual into the party, and particularly into the apparatus, the Communists see to it that the party satisfies all

his needs for community and personal life. The major needs are taken care of to such an extent that, even if the party member should lose faith, his personal attachments would keep him in the fold.

4. Great emphasis is placed on evoking in the member an emotional attachment to his "iron will." He must develop an image of self characterized by such ceaselessly repeated words as merciless, implacable, irreconcilable, ruthless, relentless, fearless, etc.

5. The party employs the member for many chores and tasks, gladly pushing him into ever more responsible and perilous assignments. It is on the basis of his behavior in tight situations, his initiative and drive as an "organizer," and his ability to instill class hatred in others, that the final evaluation of his capacity and reliability is made. These methods are strengthened considerably by more brutal forms of pressure such as the splitting up of families, keeping hostages, involvement in criminal acts, and in general the incorporation into the party of the member's entire family, or, conversely, the encouragement of liaisons and marriages between party members.

COMMUNIST COMMUNICATION THEORY

Within these various efforts, the modern tool of radio has played a great role, although older tools such as newspapers, posters, and books have not been neglected. Inside the areas under Communist control, all audiences are captive. The radios are ubiquitous and noisy, and cannot be turned off. The purpose is to prevent independent thinking, to make sure that whatever message goes into a person's mind is of an approved and planned type, and to drown out all messages which interfere with the process of conditioning.

Radio also is used on a large scale in countries outside of the Iron Curtain. While the Communists find no captive audiences for their broadcasts, they have captured numerous listeners indirectly, by repeating a limited number of slogans or symbols, provoking anti-Communist speakers into replies and arguments, proposing and opposing solutions, and making "news." Counterpropaganda, aimed at the Communists, if executed clumsily, may recruit followers into the Communist fold, simply because to refute it must pick up Communist points. The danger they must avoid is the silent treatment.

In their radio and conventional mass communications the Communists simplify and sloganize their messages, employ exaggerations, distortions, sensationalism, human-interest stories, and scapegoats, and slant the messages according to situation and target. They do not hesitate to use lies. They couch their message in an authoritative style, indicating that only they know the answers, while the non-Communists preach impractical solutions and, in addition, are inferior human beings.

Beyond this, the more or less conventional, though streamlined, propaganda technique, the Communists have developed three improvements:

1. They make a distinction between agitation and propaganda, that is, they address themselves to concrete issues and cleavages, *as well as*, to the more fundamental and enduring problems. They try to create, especially among the more intelligent audiences, an understanding of the Communist doctrine as such. At the same time they try to capitalize on the grievances and desires of any group, especially of the underprivileged type, which by force of circumstances is contemplating, or engaged in, some kind of rebellious action.

2. Far from preaching one simple gospel, and addressing it to the mentally most advanced, they present many different teachings ranging all the way from pure communism via crypto- and semi-communism to "front doctrines" and even synthetic ideologies for such unlikely customers as nationalists, conservatives, liberals, and even anti-Communists. By and large, their best target among the educated and semieducated is the frustrated intellectual whose scientific thought habits are underdeveloped. The ideal devotee of the Communist gospel is one who seeks certainty, is emotionally attached to a prejudice or a preestablished position, is unwilling to verify his preconceived notions, and has the wrong idea of objectivity.

3. The Communists combine propaganda with organization. The propagation of their messages leads necessarily to the recruitment of additional members. The new members, in turn, must participate in the wider propagation of the faith.

The Communists make the most of treating all issues in only black and white or in either-or terms, without admitting the possibility of shading. The Communists employ this device in their "social criticism" of the imperfections of the free-enterprise system. At the same time, the imperfections of the Soviet system can be glossed over by pointing out that the welfare of the masses is slowly increasing.

"Either-or" thinking, however, is less a device than an essential ingredient of Communist thought. The Communist thinks in simple alternatives, and only in them, such as friend-enemy, "who is not for me is against me," "one or the other system will win." Thinking in all-or-nothing terms ("all capitalists are . . .") is a variant of this prescientific mode of cogitating.

The Communists are adept at all kinds of semantic and sophistic chicanery. They point out that the originator of an unwelcome thought is a capitalist, a slave of capitalism or, in any event, not a proletarian and certainly not a class-conscious one. They artfully assign concrete reality to abstractions. Thus a "class" is treated as though it were an individual. The individual's reality is "determined" by his belonging to one or the other "class." The term, "capitalism," also is an abstraction; moreover, it is a generic term which covers many different economic systems.

SPECIFIC GOALS OF THE COMMUNIST EFFORT

In summary it can be said that Communist psychological warfare aims at the following objectives:

1. The creation of a psychologically strong, obedient, disciplined, steadfast, and iron-willed leadership core which thinks and behaves in a certain way, in that way only, and in that way for a long time regardless of obstacles.

2. The creation of a larger group of oriented propagandists who spread Communist notions and are instrumental in creating and maintaining a suitable frame of reference imposed upon non-Communists.

3. The creation in both groups of a burning sense of hatred.

4. Docility, discipline, and controllability of subject populations which must be commanded by the unopposed will of the party leadership.

5. The creation, in the ruling, upper, and intellectual classes of non-Communist societies, of frustration, confusion, pessimism, guilt, fear, defeatism, hopelessness, and neurosis, of lack of will, in essence the psychological destruction of anti-Communist leadership.

6. The splitting of a society into many competing and mutually hostile groups and the sapping of the spirit of loyalty, community, mutual helpfulness, positive expectation, and willingness to take risks and to act.

7. The creation and stimulation of an all-pervading sense of fear and anxiety, whether it be fastened onto the dangers of nuclear war, or physical terror, or professionl, social, and human ruin.

8. The capture of the time dimension in the sense that an expectation of cataclysm and no-progress under capitalism is established and paired with affirmed expectation that the future belongs to communism.

9. The promise of relief from all troubles by means of an infallible as well as inevitable solution.

10. The semantic domination of intellectual, emotional, and socio-political life is well as the semantic control of all political arguments.

11. The weakening and destruction of national consciences in the Free World and the inculcation of bad conscience about firm opposition to communism and the ideals usurped and distorted by it.

In former times, the Communists perhaps had illusions about their ability to convince. They expected that the great majority of all peoples would become "proletarian" in status and conscience. With these early expectations gone, it seems that the Communists have adopted a more moderate but presumably more practical objective: simply to frustrate the anti-Communists.

The rationale of zigzag tactics is to cause the opponent to build up a defense against zig, and shortly before it becomes effective, to "annul" this defense (the term is Bulganin's) by performing a zag. Thus, the initiative is slated to remain in Communist hands. The West, it is hoped, never will reach its objective successfully. As a result of the Free World's near failures, the Communists achieve mental and psychological ascendancy; in particular they prove that the stronger will is theirs. The recipe is simple: fears, guilt neuroses, lack of will power, and disoriented minds for the democracies, and fearlessness and resoluteness for a Communist elite acting with firm discipline and according to one doctrine. Psychological weakness in the Free World will then be pitted against the psychological strength of the Communist janissaries.

Much of this may be wishful thinking on the part of the Communists, but to the degree that the most crucial decision of all, war or peace, has been allowed to slip into Communist hands, the Communists have achieved psychological dominance. The Kremlin almost has become the master of mankind's fate: harsh, jealous, revengeful, and unpredictable like Jehovah—a father image the like of which the world has never seen. John Foster Dulles described this unhealthy situation as early as 1946: "Few men in political life anywhere act without first thinking whether they will please or displease the leaders of the Soviet Union. Never in history have a few men in a single country achieved such worldwide influence."

This worldwide influence is the true measure of Soviet success in psychological warfare.

The only redeeming feature is that the Kremlin Olympus is neither omnipotent nor omniscient. It is beset with its own fears and psychological difficulties, which today are increasing at a staggering rate. Its methods work only for a time and to a degree. At the height of physical power, the motivation and conviction of communism have begun to wane. The Männerbund at the top of the Communist movement has been split up, because the image of the iron-willed robot is an unreal one, because neither healthy psyches nor minds can be kept in a state of constant disorientation, and because the Communists bear a huge guilt for numerous crimes and gradually are beginning to feel the pangs of conscience.

The psychological planning of man has remained impossible. Yet we would be foolish to ignore that the Communists have made great strides in the art of psychological manipulation. The West does not yet understand the nature of the psychological attack that has been launched. It does not comprehend the causes of its paralysis, and often does not even notice that its freedom to act has been impeded. Once the Free World will assess the conflict in its psychological dimension, the course of history will be reversed.

V

U.S. PSYCHOLOGICAL AIMS [1]

Most Americans are baffled by the disturbingly frequent episodes that show dislike for America by people in many countries. Many among those who consider our propaganda ineffective do so on the basis of the observation that all over the world—even in such Free World nations as Canada or West Germany—there is much, perhaps even increasing, "unfriendliness" toward the United States.

One of the basic, widely held misconceptions is that a primary objective of propaganda is to secure "friendship" and sympathy in a general sense. Unfriendly remarks or attitudes—such as would be resented in individual relationships—are, as a matter of course, considered proof of failing propaganda.

Actually, propaganda aims not at creating benign sentiments in others, but at influencing political opinion and creating favorable political reactions. Observers of foreign reactions to America and the Americans must conclude that, indeed, millions and millions of foreigners—including those in countries occupied for years by our forces—are ineradicably convinced that we are kind, generous, helpful, more so perhaps than any other group of people. But these same foreigners may feel, and say, that we are politically naive, mercurial, overconfident, too easily dejected. Hence, even those who wish nothing better than an immigration visa to this country might be decidedly critical and often most unfriendly in their utterances and political attitudes.

The experts and specialists—inside and outside the United States Information Agency (USIA)—seem to have no doubt that, indeed, the actual objective of our overseas information effort is to be respected rather than loved. Frequently it is much more important to convey the impression that we are strong, resolved, and powerful, than that we are kind, friendly, and eminently peaceful. In any event lack of "love" for the rich and, therefore, envied United States, a superpower whose every action and omission is felt and anxiously observed in all corners of the world, could not be remedied by any amount of propaganda.

---

[1] The material in this chapter was taken from Fritz G. A. Kraemer, "U.S. Propaganda—What It Can and Can't Be," an article published in the *SRI Journal*, Fourth Quarter, 1959. Used by permission of the copyright owners.

POWER VS. WORDS

We must understand the extent to which actual realities can be overcome, in the long run, by words. The Scandinavian nations and West Germany unquestionably are profoundly anti-Communist and—because of recent or distant history—also anti-Russian. Nevertheless, they are geographically close to the Russian colossus and are small in comparison. They have the will and the desire to stay with the West, but what permits them to do so is United States power, not United States words. Deals are made by the weak with the strong, not necessarily out of love or sympathy, but frequently from fear. Should events—for example, a withdrawal of United States forces from Germany, or God forbid, the loss of West Berlin—make Russian power appear in the ascendance and United States power on the wane, the resulting loss of confidence could not be remedied by anything the USIA might do or say. The Berlin Air Lift and the naked fact of our fighting a war to save free South Korea, proved an incomparably greater propaganda asset, by demonstrating our resolve and firmness, than any paper or radio campaign. If the Arabs, who, rightly or wrongly, see in Israel their number one enemy, find that in point of fact the United States finances the existence of that enemy, while the Soviets do not, they will not be moved into our camp by propaganda.

Propaganda as an auxiliary weapon can effectively supplement the military, economic, and diplomatic weapons of a nation. But it cannot change basic factors that speak louder than words. Most certainly it is no substitute for power.

It is a widespread misconception that propaganda provides a kind of magic wand, or mysterious nostrum for influencing a worldwide target audience in any desired manner (regardless of military, economic, and political realities) such as China's growth into a world power; Sputnik; Soviet penetration into the Middle East, Africa, and even Latin America; overthrow of the pro-Western government in Iraq; the replacement of a pro-Western by an, at best, neutral government in Lebanon, *despite* the temporary deployment of United States forces in that country; the reduction of French and British, and the lagging buildup of German, NATO forces in continental Europe; the barbaric, but yet successful, suppression of the Hungarian freedom movement by Russian tanks; launching by the Kremlin of virtually ceaseless diplomatic offensives, increasingly more insolent and threatening in tone.

Those who ascribe the decrease in United States prestige and status in world opinion to an ineffective propaganda program simply attribute to the propagandist a magic power he does not possess. The prestige of this country depends—apart from short-term tactical propaganda coups—not on words but on deeds; i.e., on our actual foreign policy and the military, economic, and will power behind it.

PROPAGANDA RESULTS CANNOT BE MEASURED

Unfortunately the success of a propaganda effort cannot be "measured." If things go well in a particular area, credit is almost never given to the efforts of the USIA—and, indeed, the propagandists would be at a loss to prove that Adenauer's Germany, for example, is friendly as a result of the Agency's operations. On the other hand, if the trend of opinion and policy turns against the United States in Indonesia or the Arab countries, the propaganda apparatus will be saddled with at least part of the blame.

At almost regular intervals attempts are made, through the establishment or reestablishment of evaluation offices within the USIA, through public-opinion surveys, etc., to evaluate concretely the effect of our overseas information program. From the manner in which, each year, the USIA representatives at budget hearings search for an an answer to questions about their achievements, it is clear that these attempts have failed. Yet, it is just conceivable that one American book found on the shelves of a USIA library might give a future leader of his country his basic concepts of politics and society—as Sun-Yat-Sen was originally won for socialism by a pamphlet that chanced to come into his hands. But such "conversion," which might become politically important only 20 years hence, could not today be registered on any evaluation chart. Thus, while Congress and the public at large see the need for, and may even overestimate the possible accomplishments of, an overseas information program, they look at the whole undertaking with suspicion.

However great the suspicion toward official propaganda, as long as the Free World is faced with the Soviet threat, we will continue to maintain governmental machinery to present our case officially, authentically, systematically, to the peoples of the world. We will also, however, unless a new Korean-type war or some near catastrophic event on the international scene shocks us into a state of virtual mobilization, not appropriate any essentially larger funds for foreign information than we do now, regardless of warnings and implorations. This means that the sum total available for the USIA type of activities and for the State Department administered exchange-of-persons program will continue to range between $100 and $150 million per year.

NO CHANGE IN GENERAL CHARACTER OF U.S. PROPAGANDA

A review of the United States informational activity—the studies by governmental committees, the budget justifications, the voluminous public discussions by experts of various grades—leads inevitably to the conclusion that the kind of propaganda we are now making, and which has changed little throughout the last decade, is exactly the type of propaganda this nation is "capable" of making and which, therefore, it will continue to make.

United States propaganda has practically no choice but to follow an in-between line, to steer a careful, middle course.

The present balance is not, however, a mixture invented and prescribed by some master propagandist. It is simply a reflection of the crosscurrents of United States public, especially congressional, opinion. Faced with extreme diversity of views, the USIA cannot deviate perceptibly from its present well-established middle-of-the-road course.

We overlook basic traits of American psychology if we expect our propagandists to develop a single, succinct, dramatic doctrine. We are, for better or for worse, a pragmatic nation; we believe in developing "practical" solutions, "workable" compromises, individual roads to salvation; we are, by our temperament and our history, deeply wedded to the nondogmatic approach.

In the light of United States historical and psychological realities, it appears senseless to demand of our propagandists, or others, that they come forth with a full-fledged body of doctrine—a Capitalist Manifesto or the like—simply to counter in kind the Communist dogma. Any militant ideology presupposes a mystical sense of certainty, a fanatical fervor, an inclination to think in abstract and esoteric terms, and moreover an intolerance and one-sideness, all of which are alien to our national character. And if, perchance, anyone were, nevertheless, to set forth such an ideology, then the rigidity and dogmatism bound to go with it would make it unacceptable to the nation at large and, thus, unusable for official propaganda purposes.

The innate American aversion to any ideological or any messianic element in United States propaganda is, however, but a symptom of an infinitely broader, deeply ingrained conviction that our propaganda should be hard-headedly sober, realistic, factual, down-to-earth, and rational. Americans believe that in the ultimate analysis an appeal to reason is infinitely more powerful than an appeal to emotions, though the latter may produce temporary results. We are suspicious of flag waving; uniforms; rhetorics; preaching, as opposed to teaching; symbolism, as opposed to concrete demonstration; alleged idealistic motivation, as opposed to a frank admission of material interest. Thus we feel that it would be unbusinesslike to indulge, with taxpayer money, in any far-fetched psychological experiments.

PROPAGANDA—PRIVATE-INITIATIVE STYLE

In accordance with our firm belief in the general superiority of private over governmental initiative, strong emphasis has been given to the potential capabilities of a privately organized effort. Many insist that American individuals and organizations could supplement, or even outdo, by their own methods and in their own way, the official effort to influence opinion abroad. The classical and best-known examples are Radio Free Europe, Radio Free Asia, and Radio Liberation, all established by nongovernmental groups and maintained with essentially private funds to broadcast to the subjugated people behind the Iron and Bamboo curtains.

Our most impressive and most advertised large-scale, nongovernment program in international communications is the People-to-People Foundation, Inc., launched with great expectations and considerable publicity by President Eisenhower in September, 1956. It was an attempt to mobilize the entire nation for a coordinated, systematic effort by all major business, civic, scientific, artistic, religious, press, radio, sports, etc., groups and associations "to enlarge communications and contact between Americans and citizens in foreign lands in the interest of better understanding." The Foundations set up 41 functional committees (Advertising Organizations, Banking, Cartoonists, Fine Arts Groups, Hobbies, Nationality Groups, Radio and Television, Veterans, Women's Groups, etc.) composed of men and women recognized as top leaders in their respective fields. The Foundation was supposed to work out its own program and raise its own funds.

The virtual collapse of the People-to-People Program illustrates that the American private citizen, while always eager to aid an obviously good cause, is not a persistent missionary in the field of foreign affairs. After a burst of enthusiasm, often characteristically accompanied by the creation of ambitious plans and organizations, he turns to more concrete problems nearer home.

A sustained propaganda effort by private groups or individuals, even under glamorous and authoritative leadership from their own ranks, must not be expected. Virtually the whole burden of effort rests with the government.

The deeper problem regarding privately sponsored efforts is, however, not lack of vitality, but their very nature. Planning and operations are exclusively aimed at creating friendship, good will, understanding between United States and foreign citizens and groups. It is assumed that friendly personal contacts must, as a matter of course, generate not only personal sympathies between people but also political sympathy for the United States.

Equating generally benign sentiments with political attitudes is fallacious. The expectation that nonpolitical activities by nonpolitical individuals—neither equipped nor inclined to blend their gestures of good will with appropriate political indoctrination—will produce political results is vain.

Even more serious is the misconception that these relatively shallow public relations-type gestures could really produce any deeper or more lasting effect, political or nonpolitical, on the souls, hearts, or minds of the intended addressees. In this age where—outside the United States—uncertainty and insecurity, doubts, and despair are very marked, it takes more to move men. Above all, it requires a greater intensity and profundity.

American tourists and businessmen cannot, for similar reasons, be considered as an army of natural propagandists. Their contacts with the local population are, in the overwhelming majority of cases, superficial and limited. Few of them will be politically minded or politically articulate, or, if they are, they seldom possess the inclination and aptitude to act as political missionaries on the side—not to mention the usual language barrier. On the whole, tourists will be appreciated for economic reasons and probably be liked personally, but they will hardly change the political preferences of those with whom they come in contact. In many cases they will be considered, regardless of what they do, with the same feelings the inhabitants of Maine entertain for the "summer people."

Our commercial information media, however imposing their achievements in other fields, cannot carry the burden of propaganda. The output of commercial United States information enterprise is largely nonpolitical, to a degree that precludes any but the most marginal propaganda impact. But, political or nonpolitical, the product is tailored overwhelmingly, if not exclusively, to American needs and tastes, even where a considerable foreign market is involved. This leads to the paradox that the product of our information industry, if used on non-Americans, may be more harmful than helpful.

Our movie industry actually shuns the political field. It does not undertake the production of films, in English or foreign-language versions, aimed at the political susceptibilities of foreign groups as do the Soviets and Chinese.

The high entertainment value of American movies is in itself sometimes assumed to be a propaganda asset. But here we encounter a paradox. The popularity of United States movies for entertainment is unique, especially among the younger age groups abroad. However, they also create, among the sophisticated and the unsophisticated alike, a picture of the United States, its life, culture, tastes, and ideals that is so distorted that part of the official United.States information effort is actually to dispel the misleading image.

The Press. For somewhat different reasons, the same contradiction applies also to the American daily press, political magazines, and news services. Papers like the New York Times or New York Herald Tribune, wire services such as UPI and AP, are unparalleled in broadness of coverage and objectivity. But this very objectivity and extra ordinary range of coverage, the extreme frankness with which our foreign policy, our military strategy and, in general, our innermost doubts and designs are discussed, bewilder and disturb those who do not know American ways and tradition.

America would not be America without its free press, without its public debate of all issues, and without its unrestrained expression of opinion by all and sundry. However, this daily stream of freely flowing words does not make it easier to guide and influence the impressions and thinking of foreigners in that specific, predetermined direction that would be desirable from the propaganda point of view. On the contrary, the freedom with which we rush into print has again and again provided our enemies, especially at moments of diplomatic or military crisis, with arguments and material highly useful to them and quite damaging to United States aims and policies.

A MORE EFFECTIVE EFFORT NEEDED

Regardless, however, of the many inherent limitations to an American overseas information effort, we must not lose sight of the possibilities of improving it within its given framework. Above all, much greater emphasis should be placed on the personal approach by trained people.

Students of Communist techniques agree that Communism—in countries outside the Iron Curtain—gains adherents and followers primarily by the "direct" or "personal" approach, i.e., by working on individuals through individuals. While there are, of course, cases in which intellectuals, or even others, are won over by the mere reading of Marx' or Lenin's writings, almost invariably men or women now Communists were converted by a teacher, fellow student, coworker, relative, friend, or neighbor belonging to the Communist faith or, even more likely, by a member of the party apparatus specifically charged with recruiting.

The picture of Soviet mass propaganda seducing men by Big Lie tactics, mass hypnosis, and blatant promises of material betterment is an oversimplification. Two additional characteristics of Soviet propaganda are often not sufficiently understood: most extensive use of local elements in each country to spread the gospel; reliance on individual contacts and on calls for individual participation as a primary means to gain a more than ephemeral influence over people. Without these characteristics it is unlikely that Soviet propaganda could win so many disciples.

The truth is that, quite independently and obviously not influenced by a conscious or subconscious desire to imitate Communist methods, we in the United States have likewise arrived at the conclusion that personal contacts between our propagandists and local people are the most effective and important single means at our disposal to get our propaganda across. A characteristic statement to this effect by an American newspaper correspondent abroad is quoted in the excellent Hickenlooper Report: "One ounce of personal contacts is worth a ton of literature." We also have recognized in theory that American propaganda in any given country can really reach wider circles only if it is spread there by native advocates of our views.

It is hopeless to expect the United States Information Agency missions, operating in 80 countries with less than 1,000 U.S. citizens, to do the job. Even if this small group could devote itself exclusively to "personal contacts" it would, for purely physical reasons, be able to do so on only a very narrow front. Only a minor fraction of their time can possibly be spent on the personal-contact endeavor. This means not only that the actual number of individuals "contacted" is bound to remain very limited indeed, it means also that each contact must, of needs, be relatively brief and superficial. In the struggle for men's minds and souls, a few conversations in an office, at lunch, or over cocktails cannot produce any but minor or short-range effects.

THE IMPORTANCE OF HISTORY

There flows from American humanism and humanitarianism a belief, almost an article of faith, that human beings all over the world are very much alike, that their basic aspirations, interests, fears, and hopes are not really too different. We instinctively deemphasize in our thinking the extraordinary differences that exist in the system of values and mentality of even such closely related nations as the French and Italian. Thus we come, not in theory perhaps but in actual fact, to the conclusion that it cannot really be so very important whether, in dealing with Frenchmen or Italians, we do know their history and literature, their peculiar social stratification, their special philosophy of life—in short, their true national individuality. Americans are also more "modern" than almost any other national group, in the sense that we live in the present and look into the future. This also leads to a natural nonconcern with the underlying historical developments that have shaped those foreign nations that constitute our target audience today.

We cannot inject into our "information campaign" those elements of ideology, emotionalism, and fanaticism, or such imaginative novel techniques and bold methods as would in a powerful sweep convert Communists, overwhelm neutralists, and create waves of thought and sentiment favorable to United States objectives. But we can by a sober and persistent effort, covering—if on a limited scale—all parts of the Free World, explain our case to those not yet blinded by prejudice or resentment, dispel false notions regarding our way of life and intentions, and, most important, make it impossible for the Communist side to gain further ground unopposed.

VI

THEMES AND WORDS [1]

Nikita S. Khrushchev, prime minister of the Union of Soviet Socialist Republics and first secretary of the Communist Party of the Soviet Union, is communism's leading traveling salesman. Even though he temporarily dropped the pretense of reasonableness at the May summit meeting, he has everywhere preached disarmament, negotiation, coexistence, nonaggression and peace—all of them words sweet to our ears. For example, on February 11, 1960, he told the Parliament in India:

> It is our firm conviction that . . . all disputed international issues . . . [should be solved] through negotiations. . . . Lasting peace . . . would have a most beneficial effect upon the life of all peoples of the world. . . . The realization of a program of general and complete disarmament would usher in a new era in the development of human society—a world without wars, without the nuclear missile race. . . . I profoundly trust that the forces of reason, the forces of peace will prevail in the long run over the forces of war and will ensure humanity a happy and bright future under conditions of lasting peace and progress. . . .

But Khrushchev also has attacked "American warmongering" and he has expressed confidence that communism will "bury" capitalism. In this quote this same thought is presented in the form that "the forces of peace will prevail . . . over the forces of war."

What is Khrushchev saying? Is he talking peace or war? Why does he use a vocabulary which seems to lend itself to multiple interpretations and misinterpretations?

For the Communists, language is not just a tool for communicating ideas or a means in the search for truth. They choose words not to clarify but to produce ambiguities and induce false thinking. Strongly impressed by the usefulness of cheap and powerful weapons, they have striven to become experts in verbal artfulness. They have created a special vocabulary to serve as the cutting edge of a technique of semantic deception. Like the winds and the seas which can hollow out the hardest rock, the weapon of semantics, more subtle and less immediately destructive than nuclear bombs, has the power of eroding society. Words can serve the same purpose as artillery barrages before an attack, preparing nations opposed to communism to accept with a minimum of protest the "decisive" or death-dealing

---

[1] The text for this chapter is taken from Stefan T. Possony, "Words That Divide the World" published by the *Saturday Evening Post*, 9 July 1960. Used by permission of the copyright owners.

blow. In brief, the Communists have taught themselves to use language as an instrument of conquest.

Historically the Communist vocabulary has consisted of two types of expressions—one set for communicating with one another, the other for communicating with the rest of the world. Their standard lexicon for internal use is replete with terms like "violence" and "class warfare." It is a language of combat designed to win the struggle for the world through force, revolution and war. By contrast, their Aesopian terminology—the words employed in external communication—is derived primarily from Western political thinking and includes terms which evoke positive emotions. Communists are eager to create the impression that they are peace-loving and anxious to arrange for an international system of "live and let live." Thus, like the zebra, with its day and night barks, the Communists use different languages to accommodate different audiences.

As Communist semanticists attained virtuoso skills, they discovered that, in many instances, communication can be made to serve a dual purpose—to say one thing to Communists while simultaneously conveying quite a different message to non-Communists. To the party followers the usual communication is an instruction to revolutionary action. But this very same communication must present a soothing, attractive, pacifying, and paralyzing idea to the outside world.

This "double-think" or "double-talk" mission is accomplished by applying a practice developed more than sixty years ago by Lenin who also coined the expression "Aesopian language." Aesop, the sixth-century, B.C., Greek fabulist, invented the technique of hiding moral and political points behind seemingly innocuous stories and originated such colloquialisms as "sour grapes," "the wolf in sheep's clothing," "the dog in the manger," and "belling the cat." In his time Lenin avoided tsarist censorship of his writing by masking "communists" as "strict Marxists" and substituting "*the* reform"—not to be confused with "reforms," which was an Aesopian term dear to moderate socialists—for the taboo word "revolution."

By now most of the original Communist vocabulary has been given an Aesopian equivalent. "Dictatorship of the proletariat" grew into "democracy"; "expropriation" was transformed into "planning"; "revolution" was camouflaged as "liberation"; and "communism" itself was disguised as "anticolonialism," "antiimperialism," or "antifascism."

The present leaders of the Soviet Union frequently reiterate their firm adherence to the principles of Marx, Engels, and Lenin. This constant reassertion of allegiance to their "founding fathers" is more than a ritual profession of faith required by all true and pseudo-religions. Far more significantly, it is a reminder to Communist audiences that they must interpret all Soviet statements, even the most Aesopian, in the light of the original Communist creed.

For example, while Khrushchev may use the term "peaceful coexistence" without qualification a few times, he soon takes pains to explain that he is talking about the "Leninist concept of coexistence." Communists know that this particular concept is quite different from what most Westerners presume the word "coexistence" to mean.

Shakespeare asked: "What's in a name? That which we call a rose by any other name would smell as sweet." And that great master of the ruse, Stalin, laid down this rule: "Words must have no relation to action. . . . Words are one thing, actions another. Good words are a mask to conceal bad deeds."

The Communist conflict doctrine is simple enough, and more or less self-evident. The goal—never rescinded and frequently reiterated—is to ensure the world victory of communism; that is, to seize power anywhere and ultimately everywhere.

The concept of how Communists think they might be able to reach this goal can be summarized in three basic propositions:

ONE: There are three types of conquest techniques—the nonviolent, such as propaganda and economic warfare; the violent, such as terror, guerrilla operations and uprisings; and the military, such as civil and international, conventional, and nuclear war. Communists must master all these types of conflict and be ready to employ each and any, singly or in combination, according to necessity or opportunity.

TWO: While much can be gained from propaganda and political warfare, strong opponents can be overthrown only by force and firepower. The world cannot be conquered for communism—or for anyone—without "frightful collisions" in the form of major wars.

THREE: Although war is inevitable, every effort should be made to weaken the opponents of communism before extreme risks are taken and decisive military battles are joined. Through careful preparation the military phases of the conflict should be rendered as cheap and easy as possible. If and when the Communists achieve overpowering force superiority, the anti-Communist nations may be prevailed upon to surrender rather than risk destruction.

The Communists constantly update these simple concepts to conform to changes in technology; yet basically these ideas have remained the guiding principles of Communist behavior for half a century. They also are the key which deciphers the true meaning of Aesopian language. Let us apply this key and translate into plain English some of the catchy words which the Soviets are using to advance their fortunes.

NEGOTIATION

The Communists understand negotiation as a conflict technique facilitating conquest on the installment plan. It is a method of agitation and a tool for weakening the opponents of communism. But if genuine political issues are involved, it can never be a method for settling disputes with non-Communists. The true purpose of negotiation is to get and not to give.

The time consumed in a negotiation provides a breathing space; if a longer respite is required, an agreement may be signed. To be acceptable, agreements must have "revolutionary significance"; they must not, as Stalin put it, "hinder the Communist Party from conducting its independent, political, and organizational work . . . and from preparing the conditions necessary for the hegemony of the proletariat." Once the agreement is signed the respite achieved must be exploited "to secure future strategic advantages" (Stalin).

Agreements should be adhered to only so long as they are useful to the revolutionary cause. If agreements become onerous or impede the advance of communism, Lenin's rule applies, that Communists should not tie their hand with "considerations of formality," and treaties and compacts may be broken—without warning and without renegotiation.

All international conflicts over relations between capitalism and communism as social systems—issues like unification of Germany, "lowering of tension," disarmament, armistices, peace treaties, and so on—involve political issues. When negotiations on such problems are held with the democratic nations, the Communist intent is to gain concessions and time, and to convince the non-Communists that they must grant compromises which will lead to a "lasting" settlement of the problem. Yet no Western concession can be final before ultimate surrender. If a problem is settled by negotiation now, another must be posed immediately, and then another, in an interminable sequence.

How does the "semantic misunderstanding" resulting from projecting our meaning of negotiations into Communist statements affect international relations?

In 1958 Khrushchev declared, "We shall never settle controversial problems in relations between states by means of war. We shall endeavor to solve problems of this kind peacefully by negotiation." Like all other governments, Communist states naturally find it useful to engage in negotiations of the customary type *if nonpolitical issues are involved*. In their language, "interstate" problems must not be confused with international problems. The latter are "political" and hence important, the former deal with technical matters. In this statement, then, Khrushchev meant that the really decisive questions could not be settled by negotiation. But superficial reading conveys the opposite impression. Actually, Khrushchev promised merely to "endeavor" settlement.

The record shows that the Soviets have an excellent chance to gain from negotiations with the West. Given their definition of the term, negotiation is a game that they cannot possibly lose. By adhering strictly to their understanding of what it means to negotiate, they are free to engage in endless talk and go home without agreeing to anything, or to sign an agreement "as a means of gaining strength" (Lenin), with every intention of breaking the agreement later, as soon as it ceases to have "revolutionary significance." Hence, it is not surprising that in 1955 the Senate Judiciary Committee reported that within thirty-eight years, the Soviet Government had concluded nearly 1,000 treaties and "broken its word to virtually every country to which it ever gave a signed promise." This finding is consistent with Communist understanding of what the words "negotiation" and "agreement" mean. They acted exactly as their doctrine taught them to act.

PEACE AND PEACEFUL COEXISTENCE

The Communists define peace as the nonmilitary phases of protracted conflict. To them, peace means: (a) an invitation to non-Communists never to resist efforts to expand the Communist empire and to hasten the communization of the world; (b) the utilization of conflict methods short of war, such as propaganda, political warfare, uprising, and guerrilla fighting; (c) the creation of optimum conditions for risking military battle; (d) the terminal point of Communist world conquest; and (e), in the form of "lasting peace" the period after the consolidation of the classless society.

A "peace policy" is considered to be "merely another and—under given conditions—a more advantageous form of fighting capitalism." According to a Comintern resolution of 1928, "peace policy" provides "the best basis for taking advantage of the antagonisms among the imperialist states." The term does not imply that the Communists intend reconciliation with capitalism: "struggle for world peace" is the Aesopian term for "cold war."

"Peaceful coexistence" is the current version of "peace policy." The term denotes a temporary situation in which there is an absence of violent struggle. During such a period careful and cautious tactics should be used while preparations are being made to resume the "advance of communism."

Khrushchev has defined coexistence in a most pedestrian way. He does not "want capitalism to exist . . . but cannot help but recognize that it does exist." Yet, he warned, "if you live among dogs, keep the stick with you."

796-096 O - 65 - 6

Upon his return from the United States, a more orthodox Khrushchev explained peaceful coexistence by referring to Lenin's "flexible" foreign policy in signing the peace treaty with Germany in 1918. Lenin himself frequently cited this particular treaty as an example of how Communists could obtain a "breathing space" when they needed time. In 1925 Stalin defined "the essence of the question" as: "Who will defeat whom?" This definition applies to all conditions prior to Communist victory including "coexistence."

Whenever we transfer our American interpretations of peace and coexistence to Communist statements on the subject, misunderstanding is sure to arise.

In May 1959, Khrushchev met with a group of United States businessmen visiting the U.S.S.R. and remarked: "Do not be afraid . . . neither for yourselves nor for your children. You may sleep undisturbed, the U.S.S.R. will never use its forces to attack anyone." But by his own insistence Khrushchev is a good Communist. He does not expect that communism can be established through democratic elections. "In the process of the proletarian world revolution, wars between proletarian and bourgeois states . . . will necessarily and inevitably arise" (Lenin). Khrushchev has promised the Free World to bury it, and when he was in the United States he confirmed that he had used this expression. He explained that he did not mean to bury every American in a physical sense, a correction which he found hilarious. But he did mean, he said, that capitalism was historically doomed and that communism would prevail.

Khrushchev did not volunteer any particulars about the precise processes or procedures by which that abstraction, history, would bury the United States. In view of the hazards of nuclear war, Khrushchev probably prefers to prevail peacefully. But, so far, the Communist dictionary has never said that the Communists desire to coexist peacefully to the end of time: the book says clearly that coexistence is only for the time being.

In his farewell address to the American people on September 27, 1959, Khrushchev said: "In the Soviet Union everyone is in favor of living in peace." Of course, according to Communist doctrine, "lasting peace and progress" can be attained only after the abolition of capitalist "property relationships." Thus, so far as the Communists are concerned, lasting coexistence envisages the peculiar relationship which the dog shares with the bone and the rope with the executed.

DISARMAMENT PROPOSALS

The Communists define disarmament proposals as efforts designed to divert attention from security problems, to weaken hostile military forces quantitatively and qualitatively, and to change the world balance of power in favor of communism. Since disarmament proposals may lead to negotiations, they are conceived as a device to "buy time."

Lenin maintained that a sincere demand by Communists for disarmament is "reactionary," "illusionary," and "tantamount to the complete abandonment . . . of revolution." He taught that "every 'peace program' is . . . a piece of hypocrisy." Communists should make disarmament proposals "to recruit sympathizers . . . overthrow the *bourgeoisie*, and establish the proletarian dictatorship."

Obeying this injunction, the Communists since 1922 have made seven radical disarmament proposals, and negotiations on the subject have dragged for a generation. Late in 1959 Khrushchev, asserting that the Soviets do not want to threaten or attack anybody, personally presented a "new" disarmament plan to the United Nations— a plan which Ambassador Henry Cabot Lodge aptly described as a proposal for 100-percent disarmament and 10-percent inspection. Khrushchev's plan is inspired by the Communist definition of "general and complete disarmament." This definition indicates that a "world without wars" would constitute "a new era in the development of human society"—meaning disarmament is possible only *after* the world revolution has been accomplished.

Similarly, according to the Communist dictionary, international confidence can prevail *only* in a Communist world. This being the case, Communists "negotiate" about disarmament by arguing against control and inspection on the grounds that confidence must precede inspection. Hence, no inspection without communism; but obviously in a world empire under Communist monopoly rule, inspection would be redundant. Communist arguments about control exasperate United States negotiators; nevertheless they conform completely to Communist understanding of the words involved.

In an attempt to prove the sincerity of his disarmament proposals, Khrushchev, in January 1960, announced to the Supreme Soviet that a "major reduction" of the Soviet armed forces would be carried out. In this case, "disarmament" simply meant disbandment of troops no longer needed. For in the same speech Khrushchev stated openly that "in reducing the number of men in the armed forces, we are not diminishing firepower. On the contrary, it has increased qualitatively several times."

The Communists are faithfully executing Lenin's directive to work toward "the arming of the proletariat . . . and the disarming [of] the *bourgeoisie*." They do desire disarmament; for by their own definition disarmament before the completion of the revolution means, first, the unilateral disarmament of their opponents and, second, the strengthening of their own forces. It would seem, then, that in this case the semantic divergence between communism and the Free World is almost 180° apart.

LIBERATION MOVEMENTS AND IMPERIALISM

The term "liberation movement," if used by Communists, differs from the Western usage which became widespread during World War II and referred to indigenous forces operating against the Nazis and the Japanese in occupied countries.

Communists think of "liberation movements" as guerrilla or insurrectional forces fighting against "imperialists," "capitalist enslavers," and "national oppressors." Lenin asserted that "the liberation of the oppressed class [that is, the coming to power of the Communists] is impossible . . . without a violent revolution." Liberation movements help to create the conditions for such a revolution.

"Liberators" may be democrats or nationalists, or even reactionaries and Fascists, or they may be Communists. As Stalin phrased it, so long as these movements "weaken imperialism and contribute to its overthrow," their own political orientation matters little to the Kremlin. Sometimes it is preferable for a liberation movement not to be Communist, or to operate under an "anticommunist" label. As long as they create local unrest and disperse the forces of their opponents, movements which are potentially or actually useful to the Communists are given the honorific title of "liberation." Yet the name changes quickly if and when activist political movements perform contrary to Communist directives and interests. "Liberators" easily can be transformed into "lackeys" (of "imperialism" or "Wall Street"), and just as easily (often as result of successful infiltration) may revert to the status of "freedom fighters."

In this context, what do the Communists mean by "imperialism"? Originally they used the term to describe those capitalist powers which run colonial empires. Currently the term is used as a circumlocution for the United States, although occasionally it means any strong capitalist state.

Americans who pride themselves on being "anti-imperialists" should beware against falling into a semantic trap. The Communist definition of "imperialism" involves the strongest hostility against the United States, hence espousal of "anti-imperialism" connotes anti-Americanism to Communist ears.

WAR

The Communists think of war as a creative force of social development, "the last word of social science on the eve of each general reconstruction of society" (Marx). Lenin voiced the opinion that "great historical questions can be solved only by violence." War is defined as the "locomotive of history" and is held to be inevitable so long as communism has not achieved its ultimate destiny.

Khrushchev has pointed out that "the forms of social revolution vary." The non-Communist ruling classes "will not surrender their power voluntarily," he admits. But the degree of violence required to force their surrender will differ with the strength which a given "ruling class" possesses. Weaker states may be impelled to surrender by revolution or insurrection. To effect the capitulation of stronger states ruled by strongly willed "classes," war is needed.

Yet war is not defined in purely military terms, but involves paramilitary and nonviolent operations. "Struggle," which is the generic term, requires employment of all and any conflict techniques which could be used to advantage. Political and nonmilitary operations of all types must precede, accompany and follow combat, to minimize risks and costs, and maximize the chances of military victory. War is merely a specific form of "struggle": it is both the most violent manifestation and the decisive event in each phase of the protracted struggle between communism and capitalism.

The Communist definition of war distinguishes between "just" and "unjust" wars. "Just" wars are those which accelerate the global success of communism. "Justness" has no relation to the size or type of the war—it may be global, or it may be limited war, and it may be fought with any weapons, nuclear or conventional. "Any war . . . waged . . . with the object of strengthening and extending socialism . . . is legitimate and 'holy.' "

Communists define revolutionary wars as those in which Communist forces participate directly; these wars are "more just" than other types of just wars. Liberation wars are undertaken by allegedly oppressed peoples against their non-Communist rulers. Liberation wars also are "just," and hence Communists may lend covert or overt support to the side which wants to alter the status quo. Yet depending on changes in the international situation and in Communist policy, the Who's Who of the "just" and the "unjust" may be reversed quite suddenly; and sometimes both sides are supported to keep the pot boiling. For war itself is the thing.

By contrast, the Communists define any war fought by non-Communists as "unjust." Such wars may be imperialistic or predatory. Imperialistic wars are fought between strong non-Communist states; predatory wars are waged by strong capitalist states against weaker nations.

The question of who initiated the war has no bearing on the "justness" or "unjustness" of a conflict. This question is extremely important in Western thinking but according to Lenin's definition, wars fought by the Communists are always "just." The respective "class character" of the belligerents—which is the decisive factor—is not changed by the formalities of initiation. The choice of an offensive or defensive strategy is a technical matter directed by necessity or opportunity and does not affect the moral character of the war.

The Communist definition of aggression is closely related to their concept of "just" and "unjust" wars. According to their semantics, which bestow upon them, *a priori*, a blanket authorization for all their acts, Communists never can be aggressors—even if they initiate war. Yet a capitalist state defending itself against a direct and unprovoked attack launched by the Communists or by a "liberation movement" is necessarily an aggressor. According to this manipulation, the United States in the future never can fight a just war except—perhaps—as an ally of the Soviet Union.

For about thirty years the Communists have been advocating the signing of so-called "nonagression pacts." This advocacy is perfectly compatible with preparation for what the West would call aggressive war, not only because deception must be part of an attack pattern but also because the U.S.S.R. by definition could not violate a nonaggression pact to which it is a signatory, even if it initiated attack upon a noncommunist cosignatory itself. Most of the states with whom such pacts were concluded are now behind the Iron Curtain.

When the Communist talk about war, Americans frequently fail to comprehend the subtle points. For example, Khrushchev never tires of promising that the Soviet "armed forces will not be used . . . at any time for predatory purposes." He makes this promise in good faith, for according to Communist semantics, it would be impossible for Soviet forces to fight predatory wars. Communists engage in armed conflict for one purpose only: to defend, "strengthen and extend socialism." Hence they simply cannot fight a predatory or an "unjust" war. The significant point is that Khrushchev never has forsworn the intention to use his military establishment for those kinds of war that Communists consider to be "just" in nature. Immediately after he left the United States, Khrushchev went to Peking where he reassured a high-level party audience that while Communists continue to condemn "predatory" wars, they still "recognize" just wars and wars of liberation.

In his frequent professions of undying love for peace, Khrushchev so far has refrained from taking issue with Stalin's assertion (1952) that to make war avoidable, "imperialism must be destroyed." Nor did he ever refute Mao Tse-tung's celebrated dictum that "political power grows out of the barrel of a gun."

On occasion Khrushchev has said that under the conditions prevailing in the contemporary world, wars no longer are "fatalistically inevitable." To the Communists, looking for the easy solution, "the use or nonuse of violence in the transition to socialism" does not depend on the Soviet Union, but "on whether the exploiting classes resort to violence." Stressing that nuclear weapons and intercontinental ballistic missiles would cause tremendous destruction, Khrushchev claims—and perhaps believes—that unlike the capitalist nations, the Communist camp could absorb such havoc and survive. According to him, "a third world war could only end in the collapse of capitalism." Obligingly the new-style Communists have set themselves the task of persuading the "capitalists" that they should act like reasonable businessmen, liquidating their assets with the least loss, and not mess up the predestined revolution with nuclear bombs.

Yet, despite their hope that the specter of nuclear holocaust will frighten the Free World into bloodless surrender, the Communists continue to profess that as the final showdown draws near, the capitalists, in an attempt to preserve their system, may "lash out like a wounded beast." To guard against this eventuality, they have formulated a military doctrine of "pre-emption." This is not identical with the Western concept of "preventive war," but is an attack to forestall an attack. Ostensibly a defensive concept like a parry in fencing, it could be used to justify plainly aggressive moves.

As will be remembered, even if the Communists were to initiate war against the United States, they still would not hesitate to proclaim the "justness" of this adventure in tragedy. By their own definition, an all-out nuclear attack by the Soviet bloc to kill a huge part of the American people, an assault launched to cause the final collapse of capitalism, would usher in the *most just war of history*. Regardless of how devastating such war could be for the Soviet Union itself, this supreme and deadly struggle is considered by the Communists to be both necessary and inevitable unless surrender can be induced. To the Communist way of thinking such a war, however costly, would be the indispensable high road to that type of "lasting peace"—"without the nuclear missile race"— which the Communist system alone is able to provide to "all peoples of the world."

These few examples show that to understand the Communists, we must apply *their* definitions, not our own. Communist and non-Communist conceptions of the same terms differ. Not infrequently meanings are completely at variance.

The purpose of semantic warfare is to mislead the Free World about the true objectives of communism and in particular to make believe that the Communist movement—which plans to liquidate its opponents, to destroy democracy, and to abolish political, economic, intellectual, religious, cultural, and personal freedoms—has humanitarian and progressive motivations.

The creation of illusions is an accepted part of politics. What is our defense against Communist myth-making? The true doctrine of communism has remained an open book for more than a hundred years. Even Aesopian language can be freely interpreted, because

Aesopian terms always retain some relationship to the concepts they are supposed to camouflage. Though the Free World is sometimes deceived, more often the Free World deceives itself with the wishful thought that Communists have suddenly ceased to be Communists.

If the Communists really had changed, they would be eager to explain their new doctrine; they would find persuasive words to disclose the new outlook; and they would be compelled to explain the doctrinal changes in detail to the international movement and the rest of the world. Yet they reiterate frequently that they remain committed to the original writ.

Thus, Americans have no choice but to become familiar with the Aesopian technique. Communists rely upon a few dozen texts of key importance to motivate, condition, and obligate the faithful and to explain the Communist doctrine of protracted conflict. Protective semantic analysis involves asking questions such as these: Is a given Communist statement consistent with basic Communist doctrine? Are the Communists employing expressions which amplify, modify, or limit terms Americans are using in our own political conversation? Can we find the qualifications and modifications that apply to the Communist usage of a given term? What are the original doctrinal Marxian terms which the Aesopian word replaces? Has the term previously been used to deceive? Is the particular line of arguments addressed to *high* party audiences or to nonparty forums, or to both—and if so, what is the difference in the message?

The Communists are trying to entrap us by the words we like best. They are attacking democracy where it is weakest: in its predilection for wishful thinking. In the words of Noel Coward, "It is discouraging to think how many people are shocked by honesty and how few by deceit." In order to fight the battle on even terms, we must become even more skillful in translating Communist double-talk. The Free World must learn to face the totalitarian menace without illusion.

VII

FOREIGN POLICY: SOME PSYCHOLOGICAL CONSIDERATIONS [1]

In 1871, when Prussian armies had cut off and surrounded the city of Paris, the question of the hour was: "When will the bombardment begin?" The thought of shells landing in the center of the French capital aroused a sense of dread and apprehension not unrelated to the fear that more terrible new weapons have aroused since. "When will the bombardment begin?" The question jerked at the already ragged nerves of the Parisians and was echoed throughout the capitals of the Western world. An answer—or an answer of a sort—came from Otto von Bismarck, Chancellor of Prussia. He growled: "The bombardment will start at the psychological moment."

Bismarck is only one of a long line of distinguished statesmen through history who have appreciated what may be called the psychological aspect of foreign policy. Napoleon made use of the principles of the French Revolution in extending his sway over most of Western Europe. Napoleon's armies were magnificently led and well equipped. By themselves they would have been more than a match for the forces of the old order. As protagonists of the ideas of liberty, equality and fraternity they were irresistible. Woodrow Wilson's Fourteen Points, which are often credited with hastening the disintegration of the Kaiser's Reich in 1918, provide another classical example of psychological warfare. The Fourteen Points did not cause the German armies to break ranks and flee, but they greatly strengthened the hand of German political leaders who wished to make peace. In our own time Winston Churchill has shown an outstanding ability to conceive policies which lay hold on the imagination and to state these policies in a manner which assures them of a hearing throughout the world. Both the Nazis and the Soviets have, from time to time, displayed considerable expertness in exploiting psychological vulnerabilities of their opponents.

If ability to take into account the psychological aspect of policy in war or peace can help to achieve success, maladroitness along the same lines can smooth the path to disaster. Hitler's treatment of Russian civilians in conquered areas as sub-humans may not by itself

[1] This chapter was contributed by Hans Speier and W. Phillips Davison of RAND Corporation, Santa Monica, California, to the earlier volume of 1955. It has been retained in this compilation because of its continuing value.

have lost the war for him but it added immeasurably to the problems of his outnumbered troops on the eastern front. Similarly, the aggressive and peremptory tone adopted by the Soviet Union during the time it was consolidating its gains after World War II seemed almost as if it must have been calculated to inflame the West and forge it into a defensive coalition.

THE NATURE OF FOREIGN POLICY GOALS

In order to clarify what we mean by the psychological aspect of international affairs let us first say a few words about the aims of foreign policy. It is apparent that the goals which we try to reach by means of foreign policy may lie far in the future or be close at hand. It will be convenient to speak of long-range, middle-range and short-range goals. Similarly, the aims of foreign policy may be more or less general in scope: there are many specific objectives, changing rather rapidly as time passes, as there are a few general goals which remain fairly constant. For instance, one of the cornerstones of United States foreign policy is to prevent international communism from extending its sway over any more of the Free World. This is a general goal having no limits either geographically or temporally. A middle-range, more limited goal is to create and maintain in Western Europe a strong defensive coalition. Short-range, specific goals include the ratification of the necessary international agreements by the nations concerned, the provision of given defense forces with specified weapons, and the establishment of certain joint staffs.

Our general foreign policy goals are rooted in the ideals and traditions of our country. They are formulated from time to time by the President and the Congress. Middle-range goals are usually defined by specialists within governmental agencies and are then given the stamp of approval by the Congress and the President. The North Atlantic Treaty Organization, the South East Asia Treaty Organization, the Rio Pact, the Technical Assistance program and the Atoms for Peace program are examples of instrumentalities which have been set up to help achieve certain middle-range goals. The clarity and astuteness with which these middle-range goals are formulated usually make the difference between an effective foreign policy and one which is principally composed of empty phrases. A nation may have the highest aspirations, or general goals, but unless these are given expression by clearly formulated, more limited objectives it is unlikely that they will ever be attained.

Finally, our foreign policy includes a multitude of very specific short-range goals. Some of these are fairly important and may come to the attention of the Chief Executive and the Congress. Others may be defined by the Secretary of State or by a member of his staff without recourse to higher authority. Some represent way stages on the road to the attainment of middle-range goals, but many are reactive in character. That is, they become stated because of an action taken by a foreign power. For example, when an American is unjustly imprisoned by a foreign state it usually becomes a specific goal of our foreign policy either to secure a modification of this other country's policy or to retaliate in some fashion.

Prior to World War II a large part of our foreign policy was made "on the cables" in the Department of State. By this it is meant that many decisions were made only when it was necessary to cable instructions on a specific matter to an ambassador or other national representative abroad, often in response to a query which had just arrived. These decisions then became precedents and guided the Department in sending out cables to other representatives. Under these circumstances, the bulk of our foreign policy amounted to the sum total of the individual decisions made on a multitude of relatively minor matters.

One of the great changes which World War II brought about on the American scene is that foreign policy is now made "on the cables" to a smaller extent than before. Of course, there will always be matters which require special decisions, but we now have more middle range policies and these are more clearly formulated than was ever before the case in our history. Even our general aspirations tend to be more clearly defined. In other words, there is now more planning devoted to foreign policy. Instead of only reacting to actions initiated by others, we now try and look ahead and exercise as much control as possible over the events of the future.

This development is a consequence of two basic facts. One is that American leadership in the world has grown to a point where it can possibly be contested only by one other power. This so-called bipolarity of international affairs, which has taken the place of the formerly traditional balance of power among many nations, permits no indifference toward any area of the world and allows political improvisation only at the cost of severe damage to the national interest. The other basic fact is the existence of new weapons which can devastate whole areas and paralyze nations at very short notice or at no notice at all. In the presence of thermonuclear weapons a purely "reactive" foreign policy is likely to be a foreign policy of suicide.

TYPES AND INSTRUMENTS OF POWER IN INTERNATIONAL RELATIONS

If we now look more closely at the actions we take in order to reach the goals of our foreign policy it is apparent that we act not in a political vacuum but in a world in which other sovereign powers pursue their own policies. Some of these can be reconciled with our actions; others actually help us reach our objectives: still others, however, conflict with our interests. In no case can we act freely as we could if we ruled the world. Although we do not aspire to such dominion ourselves, we are definitely interested in ensuring that no other power acquires such control over us and our friends. Instead, we plan to deter others who intend to expand their domain, and to meet pressure with resistance.

Furthermore, we are more secure if the moral and political values we cherish are at least respected, if not actually shared, in foreign countries as well. Thus forced to act in a world in which others have a measure of power themselves and are engaged in the pursuit of their own political objectives, we cannot rely on good will or the existence of a pre-established harmony, but must use whatever power and skills we have for overcoming resistance on our way to the political goals we as a nation consider just and right.

The power which can be exerted by a nation in the conduct of its foreign policy may be divided into two major classes. We may use whatever control we have over our environment and resources in order to influence the political responses of foreign governments by *external pressure or inducement*, or we may seek to utilize the existing *internal forces* which are present in others to motivate the political response we desire. We are primarily interested in manipulating the éxternal environment when we take economic measures at home, provide economic aid abroad, or engage in preclusive buying and other means of economic warfare. Mobilization of our resources for military ends, the deployment of forces-in-being, the acquisition of air bases abroad, and other categories of military action, similarly represent efforts to influence others by changing the external environment. Finally, the forming of coalitions with other powers whose interests can be reconciled with ours represents rearrangement of political power in the world in which we move. Among free countries such coalitions are restricted to circumscribed spheres of action—a military alliance, a trade treaty, an *ad hoc* agreement or a formal protest against foreign violation of international law.

Utilization of *internal forces* is exemplified by the persuasive efforts of diplomats at negotiations or at international conferences and by international mass communication. Diplomacy is not only an instrument of interaction of the nation as a whole with other nations by means of legitimate representation, but it may also be understood as an attempt to influence by means of direct communication the estimates, intentions and specific responses of individuals in foreign countries who make decisions in the field of international relations. Diplomacy is skillful if it takes into account both the ability of the representatives of foreign powers to be reasonable in the face of facts and their inclinations toward prejudice and other forms of irrationality. Like diplomacy, international propaganda attempts to help us achieve foreign policy goals by taking advantage of internal forces, but unlike diplomacy such propaganda addresses itself primarily, though not exclusively, to the masses of the foreign population.

The psychological aspects of international affairs can perhaps be understood best if we visualize a government which tries to pursue its foreign policy without diplomatic persuasion and propaganda. The instruments of economic and military power would still be used to change the environment in the double hope of improving thereby the power position of this nation *vis-a-vis* all contestants on the international scene and of influencing the immediate political responses as well as the estimates and intentions of foreign governments. It is precisely this latter influence which constitutes the psychological component of foreign policy. Once this is clearly understood, diplomatic persuasion and international propaganda are easily recognized as skills which may be used to exploit conditions which are created by the more massive instruments of power. As will be pointed out in more detail later, these skills must, of course, be employed with a view to the special psychological characteristics of the persons and groups addressed.

The conduct of foreign affairs does not exhaust itself, however, in moves and countermoves involving goods and services, military force and international coalitions. Each government tries to influence other governments not only by what it does but also by intimating, announcing, and permitting to be inferred what it might do in the future. All governments are interested in arousing *expectations* as to what they will or might do. For example, prior to the outbreak of World War II, Hitler announced his peaceful intentions after each new expansionist triumph and he always declared that the latest conquest would be his last. Like estimates of the current situation which intelligence agencies prepare for the use of those who make decisions in foreign policy, expectations about the future political moves of others are in part derived from past records in international affairs. In part, however, such expectations are derived from formal policy declarations; i.e., from words rather than actions, and from subtler indicators, such as studied chance remarks in diplomatic circles, changes in propaganda, and the like.

In this way, diplomatic skill or persistent propaganda efforts may add substantially to national power. Indeed, a diplomatic success or a propaganda campaign which weakens the hold of the foreign government over its people may have political, economic, and military implications. The opposing government may modify its policy or be replaced; public opinion in neutral countries may cheer such a change, and so on. In short, diplomacy and international mass communication also serve a double function, just as do shifts in economic or military power. They render articulate and intensify the desired psychological effect of external pressures and inducements, and they can produce effects in the same desired direction by diplomatic or other communications with foreign audiences which are *not* backed up by shifts in power. Even so, they may be effective because they shed some light on the obscure future, because they form expectations and are capable of modifying estimates of intention. For example, a dictator may behave in a friendly manner toward the ambassador of a foreign country at a reception with the purpose of having this friendly behavior observed by the representative of another power so that the latter will yield in a deadlocked negotiation with the dictatorial power. Similarly, a propaganda campaign may have political or military implications, as was true of World War II Communist propaganda in favor of establishing a "second front" as early as possible. The slogan was so persistently used by Soviet diplomacy and international propaganda against the West that the Soviet Union appeared to have been carrying the main burden of the war against Hitler all along, whereas she had been allied with Nazi Germany for nearly two years of the war and shared the spoils of war until Hitler invaded Soviet territory and established—the second front in the Soviet Union.

To repeat, actions that change the environment by redistributing international power in some form may be supported by communications about these actions in order to help steer political responses, estimates, expectations, and intentions in the desired direction. These communications, however, may at times have the effect of a real change in the distribution of power, although they are "symbolic" in nature. Political, economic, and military measures always have "psychological" implications, and diplomacy and international propaganda may at times have specific political, economic, or military implications.

ACTIONS HAVING PSYCHOLOGICAL IMPLICATIONS

The principal ways in which various instruments of power may be used to achieve a foreign policy goal may be seen by referring once more to the siege of Paris in 1871. With Prussian armies surrounding the city there were three principal courses of action open to Bismarck and his generals. They could engage in economic warfare and starve the city into submission, they could employ their military power and blast it to bits with artillery, or they could attempt to utilize the jealousies, fears, and other tensions within the beleaguered city in a variety of ways. For instance, they could negotiate with the French leaders in hopes of persuading them that resistance in the face of superior forces was futile. Or they could utilize the Parisian fears of starvation and bombardment—possibly combined with offers of generous treatment in the event of surrender—in order to demoralize the defenders of the city and undermine the authority of the government. As a matter of record, the Prussians used a combination of all these methods.

A more recent example of a category of action which combines military, economic, and psychological aspects is provided by our offshore military procurement program. In accordance with this program, the United States orders some of the military equipment which is needed by overseas military installations from factories located in foreign countries. The military and economic aspects of this program are obvious: the defensive forces are strengthened and the economy of the country filling the orders tends to benefit. Perhaps less obvious, but nevertheless present, are the psychological aspects of the action. The fact that the United States is procuring military supplies in this manner may have a variety of politically significant meanings to persons in the foreign countries supplying the goods and also in other countries.

These meanings will depend not only on the information which people receive about the procurement program, but also on their social and psychological characteristics. Those who are favorably disposed toward the United States may see the offshore procurement program as another example of the way in which we are attempting to assist friendly nations in developing strength to resist Communist encroachment. Others may prefer the Communist interpretation that this is a case of American economic imperialism. Still others, who would like to preserve their freedom but have feared that compromise with the Soviet colossus was inevitable, may view this American action as an indication that the United States will take an active interest in the defense of weaker nations, and may find courage to uphold their independence more stoutly.

The interpretation which any individual adopts will tend to make a difference in his behavior; for instance, in the behavior of the worker who is trying to decide whether or not to strike, in that of the business man who is debating whether or not to invest more money in his enterprise, and in that of the government official who is wondering whether he should or should not make overtures to the Soviet Union as "reinsurance" against the possibility of a new period of American isolationism.

The various aspects of actions taken in the conduct of foreign relations can be observed not only in dealings among nations. They can be seen—possibly more clearly—in the relations between smaller entities such as American military bases overseas and their environments. The commander of a military installation overseas has not only to take actions which will preserve and increase the military effectiveness of his forces and to see that they receive logistical support; he must also, in effect, maintain diplomatic relations with the local authorities of the host nation, region, or town and he must carefully consider the effects which his actions are likely to have on various groups within the host nation. When American forces are withdrawn from an outlying post, the local inhabitants will inevitably speculate whether this means that they are to be abandoned in the event of a Soviet attack. When military maneuvers are announced, local farmers are likely to conjure up images of trampled fields, broken fences, and frightened cattle. Sometimes as small an event as a jeep stopping outside a given building will start a rumor that the building is to be requisitioned and will give rise to a chain of actions which can damage relations between overseas military personnel and the local community.

Many overseas commanders have recognized the important psychological implications which their actions can have and have taken measures to lessen the unfavorable consequences of these actions and to increase the favorable effects. Relocation of personnel, maneuvers, and requisitioning are all necessary military activities, but they can be conducted in such a way as to take into account the feelings of the local community or in such a way as to disregard these feelings. Some commanders utilize informal committees of local citizens to advise them. Many of them take pains to see that, within the limits of military security, the local community is informed of all decisions which might affect the citizenry.

With respect to maneuvers, for example, it is common for the area affected to be announced before rumors have time to spread, and for the procedure to be specified by which farmers may secure prompt and generous compensation for any injury to their property caused by the maneuvers. In areas where requisitioning of property is still the practice, the decision as to what properties should or should not be designated for military use has been turned over to local authorities. Educational programs designed to familiarize American military personnel overseas with local conditions and customs are now the rule rather than the exception. All such actions of overseas commanders reflect their awareness that the attitudes and behavior of local communities will tend to make performance of the military mission more easy or more difficult, and that the actions taken by overseas forces will tend to affect such attitudes and behavior.

We may conclude, then, that all major actions in international relations have psychological implications and can be psychologically sound or unsound. A foreign policy which is psychologically sound attempts to maximize the desirable effects of action and minimize the undersirable effects in such ways as the following: by taking account of the social and psychological characteristics of politically significant groups abroad; by considering questions of optimum timing and surprise in the light of these characteristics; by paying attention to the possibility of exploiting initial successes; or by permitting or not permitting another power to save face. In these and similar ways, the political strategist attempts to supplement military and economic power by taking advantage of existing social and psychological forces to influence the behavior of various individuals and groups abroad in a desired direction.

SOME MISCONCEPTIONS

Among the many misconceptions about the nature and role of psychological aspects of foreign policy are two which have been particularly harmful. One of these is that it would somehow be dishonorable to use what we know about the social or psychological characteristics of people in friendly powers in order to influence their behavior. We do not like to be manipulated, to have foreign governments take advantage of our weaknesses or special characteristics in order to induce us to act the way they want, and therefore we resist the idea of trying to influence the behavior of friendly nations by such "underhanded" means. When we speak of "manipulation" or of "underhanded means," however, we thereby prejudice the question. With equally sound (or rather unsound) logic we could ask the question in the following way: "Is it proper, in the course of our international relations, to show consideration for the feelings and the national pride of friendly peoples?" The answer, of course, is that it would be improper *not* to show such consideration. While it is unnecessary to state the problem in such extreme terms, it is clear that as long as we act with openness toward friendly nations, and as long as our policies do not violate their national interests, they are likely to welcome the attention we pay to their social and psychological characteristics.

The proposition that it is not necessarily objectionable to take account of the psychological aspect of foreign policy when dealing with friendly nations can perhaps be tested best by turning the situation around and trying to imagine our own reaction to efforts to influence behavior in the United States. Let us consider a minor example. A recent British Ambassador endeared himself to a substantial portion of the American public by familiarizing himself with the game of baseball. He was seen at Ebbetts Field; he learned the appropriate terms with which to describe batters, pitchers, and umpires, and the occasions on which to use these terms. The American press reported his rather un-British behavior with obvious relish.

Now, it would seem very probable to students of political behavior that the Ambassador's interest in baseball was not due exclusively to the fascinating character of the game—although he may have become a true fan after a period of exposure—but was due much more to the fact that baseball is a prominent feature in American life. By showing an interest in baseball, the Ambassador tended to increase his popularity with the American public. We may surmise further that the Ambassador did not pursue popularity for its own sake, but sought it because it has been the announced policy of both Conservative and Labour governments in Britain to maintain close and cordial relations with the United States. This cordial relationship—again—is not an end in itself, but is one of the ways in which Great Britain seeks to assure that America does not withdraw once more into isolationism. Thus the Ambassador's appearance at Ebbetts Field may have been a modest effort to utilize social and psychological forces in the United States to further British policy. Since this Britsh policy objective was well known and since the actions taken by the Ambassador were aboveboard, there are few Americans who would find reason to take exception to this instance of political manipulation.

One may note briefly in passing that the Soviet press has also showed considerable interest in baseball in recent years. When news reached Moscow that American troops stationed in Germany were teaching the game to youngsters in communities near military posts, Communist scribes proceeded to describe "beizbol" as a particularly bloodthirsty activity designed to foist covert military training on the peace-loving peoples of Europe. Obviously, the Soviet Union was seeking to take advantage of American characteristics in a different manner.

It is not difficult to think of a different category of instances in which attempts to influence our behavior—whether by psychological or by other means—would cause serious difficulties. We would resent it if one of our allies chose to back a particular candidate for American political office, and our allies are equally likely to object to American intervention in their domestic affairs. In a few instances it has been United States policy to take an official interest in the internal politics of friendly states, but these have been strictly circumscribed. During the Italian election campaign of 1948, for instance, the United States appealed to Italians to vote for non-Communist candidates. We did not, however, back one democratic party as against another, and any attempt to do so would very probably have backfired. As long as efforts to influence the behavior of people in friendly nations by taking account of their social and psychological characteristics are open and in good taste, they can serve to strengthen relations rather than to weaken them.

In our own interest we should hope that friendly nations will follow policies that are psychologically sound with respect to ourselves. If they are willing to take account of American characteristics and preferences when it comes to their own tariffs and their actions respecting freedom of religion and the press, for example, and are willing to refrain from actions and statements which would injure American national interest or pride, then it is the whole Free World which benefits.

In this connection it may be useful to take note of the relationship between the psychological objectives of a given policy and subversion. Subversion of the government in another state—that is, undermining the authority of that government over the people in the country—may be a goal of foreign policy under certain conditions. During wartime, more than in times of peace, it is likely to be one of the basic objectives with reference to enemy states; during peacetime it may be a policy goal in the case of an unfriendly state, although it will probably not be stated so unequivocally as it would be during wartime. To undermine the authority of the government of another state from within, a nation may use a variety of means: it may employ agents to smuggle in arms; it may try to dislocate the other state's economy by flooding it with counterfeit currency; it may negotiate secretly with a dissident group within the enemy state; or it may attempt to promote dissatisfaction with their own government or form of government among the citizens of the country. Thus, all types of policies may be used to achieve the goal of subversion; an effort to make use of existing motivations to induce subversive activity may or may not be made.

It should also be noted that psychological, as well as other measures, may equally be employed to strengthen the position of a government or a political system. At the end of World War II, for example, it was our announced policy to help the people of France secure a stable government of their own choosing. To this end we attempted to give assurances to the French people, by actions and by words, that we would respect and cooperate with any government which they chose to constitute.

The reason why acceptance of the idea that a psychological approach may be used in our dealings with friendly peoples is particularly important, and why the misconception that this approach should be used only toward enemy nations is especially damaging, is that our friends are in any event much more likely to heed our wishes and to do things which we ask them to do than are our enemies. An American official who directed a large portion of our propaganda effort during World War II said later that he considered our efforts to maintain morale in occupied countries to have been much more effective than our attempts to demoralize the enemy. For the most part enemy nationals were suspicious of our words and intentions, while the French and Polish underground fighters, for example, were eager to hear from us and were predisposed to heed our appeals for action.

And today a sound psychological approach toward our friends can make a significant contribution toward healing old divisions in the Free World and ensuring that new ones do not appear. By the same token, mistakes made in dealing with our friends can be expensive.

A second major misconception is that by manipulating the psychological predispositions of a foreign power we can somehow avoid the sacrifices which are necessary in order to employ other types of action. The argument has been advanced in some quarters that if we made a greater effort to follow the psychological approach we could spend less on armaments and economic assistance. This would be something like telling an executive in an automobile factory that if he spent more on advertising and public relations he would be able to cut down on production. The purpose of our foreign propaganda and other psychological measures, as with the public relations program of a corporation, is to see that we gain the greatest possible benefit from the actions we take. It is probable that in the long run we will save dollars if we take into account the probable behavior of other people when we decide on a course of action, just as in the long run an able public relations program will benefit a corporation financially. But no amount of psychological expertise will enable any U.S. agency to hypnotize the Soviet divisions stationed in Eastern Europe or the Communist agents in Indochina. Neither will it conjure up fully armed divisions in Western Europe.

We can, however, achieve modest but worthwhile effects if we use everything we know about the internal motivations of the people who belong to politically significant groups abroad. We can use all the knowledge at our disposal about the Soviet Union and her satellite auxiliaries in our efforts to demonstrate to them that continued aggression would entail more disadvantages than advantages. We can also try and give assurances to friendly nations that they will not stand alone if attacked, and that we have a genuine concern for their political freedom, their military strength, and their economic prosperity. In the pursuit of objectives of both types, actions speak louder than words, but we can usefully employ words to supplement our military, economic, and diplomatic actions.

Development of expertise in dealing with the psychological aspects of policy has been delayed by exaggerated expectations of what can be accomplished in this manner. Too often, disappointment has led to abandonment of any attempts to make use of internal motivations at all. During World War II, some military commanders were led to believe that enemy troops would surrender if only cleverly worded leaflets were dropped on them. They found, of course, that well led and well supplied troops were unlikely to surrender no matter how skillful the propaganda appeals. As a result these commanders sometimes dismissed psychological warfare altogether. More realistic advice would have pointed out in advance that when enemy troops are cut off, decimated, and subjected to heavy bombardment, psychological warfare may in some cases be able to convince them that their position is hopeless and that they will receive good treatment and retain their honor if they surrender. Under such conditions, some enemy personnel will be likely to heed the appeal, particularly if they are not only told that they had better surrender but are also shown as specifically as possible how to go about surrendering. Psychological warfare against troops has never proved to be a substitute for military action, but has rather been a means of securing a modest but worthwhile advantage from military action which has to be taken in any case. A similar generalization might be made about other political actions which have an important psychological aspect.

THE ROLE OF INTERNATIONAL COMMUNICATION

International communication, whether it is called propaganda or information, or whether it takes place in connection with diplomacy, is an indispenasble instrument for use in any attempt to induce given attitudes or behavior in a given population. When used in this manner, international communication has two vital tasks: to bring certain actions, events, and ideas to the attention of specified audiences throughout the world, and to interpret the meaning of these actions, events, and ideas to these audiences in a designated manner.

These two tasks are at the same time ambitious and limited. They are ambitious because in order to discharge them efficiently an immense physical apparatus is necessary, an even more extensive body of accurate information about societies in all parts of the world is required, and a large corps of highly trained personnel is indispensable. They are limited because they seem to exclude the agency engaged in international communications from two major fields of endeavor—the origination of ideas and the origination of action. The positive and negative implications of these tasks will be discussed in greater detail below.

One way in which to study the part which international communication plays in foreign relations is to examine a specific event or program. United States economic assistance to Europe will serve as a case in point. When Marshall Plan goods were delivered to European countries in 1948, the *fact* of these deliveries and the *significance* of the deliveries had to be brought to the attention of large numbers of people. In this case it was appropriate to use all information media, both those directed toward the masses and those appealing to more specialized groups. Radio broadcasts, press releases, films, posters, speakers, and even diplomats attending social functions—all were pressed into service. Through all these media it was emphasized that the program of economic aid represented an effort by the United States to do her share in building a cooperative defense against further Soviet advances.

Meanwhile, Communist media throughout the world denounced the Marshall Plan as an effort of the American imperialists to dispose of surplus goods, prevent a depression in the United States, and bring about the economic enslavement of Europe. The media at the disposal of the United States hastened to combat this interpretation, not by contradicting it directly (this is a bad propaganda tactic whenever it gives a high measure of publicity to the charge of your opponent), but by trying to ensure that people knew the real aims of the economic aid program and the true facts about it.

Much more important than our own efforts in this connection was the assistance given by media of communication in friendly countries. Relatively few people saw American news releases or heard the Voice of America by short wave from New York, but numerous French, Italian, and other editors and radio men saw to it that the extent and the significance of the program of economic aid were brought to the attention of their regular readers or listeners. In the parliaments of the free nations there were representatives who were able to tell the same story and to refute the charges of Communist deputies.

This example illustrates one of the most important principles of international political communication—that it is desirable somehow to tap the media on which people customarily rely for their information, rather than to impose information from without by using foreign media. This rule of thumb does not hold, however, if the familiar, domestic media of communication are considered to be untruthful—a situation which often prevails in totalitarian countries.

Another example of utilizing an established communication network occurred during World War II, when Allied radio broadcasters spent considerable effort in sending news at dictation speed to the peoples of occupied Europe. General Bor, the principal resistance leader in Poland, has told in his memoirs how his organization monitored certain of these broadcasts and then used the information to compose leaflets and newspapers which were distributed through the Polish underground organization. More prosaic peacetime examples of this same principle may be found by observing the activities of press relations personnel of almost any embassy. These men and women are concerned primarily not with handing out information but with establishing good working relationships with the local press. If they are successful in this task the local press will, in effect, do their information work for them. Not long ago a member of the U.S. Embassy staff in a small but friendly European country was reported by a third party to be so well liked that there was not a single prominent non-Communist journalist in the country who would write an article about the United States without first checking with this embassy official to get his advice. In Washington there are a number of representatives of foreign powers who are similarly trusted by members of the American press and who thus are able to do the job of interpreting their countries' policies more effectively.

The communication expert who reaches the most people is not necessarily the most successful. The problem is to reach the right ones and at the right time. During World War II, Allied propagandists planted subtle suggestions in broadcasts beamed to Europe that German Air Force personnel were deserting. The propagandists did not believe that in this way they could actually cause enemy airmen to desert, but they knew that the German high command was monitoring Allied broadcasts and that these hints of disloyalty in the air force would cause investigations and tightened security regulations which would tend to interfere with the efficiency of operations. The audience aimed at in this case was thus a small group of high officials.

Similarly, many of our peacetime policies, and quite important ones, affect only a relatively few people abroad directly. For instance, it would be foolish to try and explain some of the complicated provisions of our tariff policy to the average radio listener or newspaper reader throughout the world. The people who need to understand these provisions in detail are relatively few in number, but they are very important. Therefore, it becomes the task of the communication specialist to find out who the people are who should receive this information, to make sure that they receive it, and to try to ensure that they do not misinterpret is meaning.

The second function of the communication specialist—that of interpretation—is less well understood but equally important. We often say that actions speak louder than words. They do, but they may say different things to different people. Troubles which we have with our allies, for example, are caused not only by what we actually do or say but also by the meanings which rightly or wrongly they attribute to these actions or words. In 1946, Secretary of State Byrnes, speaking in Western Germany, announced that the United States would favor going ahead in reconstructing German economic unity even if four-power agreement could not be obtained. This statement was widely misunderstood in France, where numerous observers felt that it portended a shift in United States policy which would be unfavorable to the French. As a result, the Secretary of State gave a further policy explanation in Paris shortly thereafter.

Whenever United States air or naval units appear in one or another part of the world the question is asked: What does this mean? Does it mean that the Americans expect trouble? Do they want to assure the Soviets that they will defend this area if it is attacked? Is it a routine training mission? Unless our communications provide an interpretation—and a convincing one—it is likely that groups abroad will ascribe a variety of meanings to the American move, and some of these meanings may tend to induce behavior unfavorable to the interests of the United States. We may be sure in any case that the Communists will interpret the move even if we are not ready to do so.

An example of the importance of interpreting military actions may be given from recent experience in Germany. A small American air force unit was moved out of a base which was only a few miles from the Soviet zonal border. The German inhabitants of the region immediately began to speculate about the meaning of this. The conclusion that many of them jumped to was that the Allies would not try to defend this area if the Soviets attacked. This conclusion, in turn, tended to strengthen the existing tendency for German businessmen to avoid establishing any enterprise near the Soviet zonal border, which had already resulted in the creation of an economically depressed band on the eastern border of West Germany. As a matter of fact, however, this interpretation of the American move did not gain substantial ground because the American authorities concerned pointed out that the move had been made in the interest of greater military efficiency. It would result not in less defense, but in better defense, because the aircraft which had previously been based in the forward area would now, in the event of an emergency, enjoy greater maneuverability from their rear bases. This announcement also pointed out that the forward base was being maintained in operational condition and would continue to be used for a number of military purposes.

While it is the primary task of communication media to report and to interpret the policies and actions of their own nation, it is a vital subsidiary task to report and interpret those of other nations as well. This is particularly true in the case of unfriendly states. Factual descriptions of the behavior of Soviet troops when they broke into Western Europe at the end of World War II have been a major factor in convincing Western Europeans that they should keep their defenses in good repair. When we learn that the Soviets are persecuting Mohammedan or other religious minorities within the Soviet Union, it is considered good propaganda tactics to ensure that this news is factually reported throughout the Middle East.

It is often necessary for communication networks in the Free World to interpret Soviet moves as well as to report them. When, for example, the Kremlin makes one of its periodic calls for an international conference to end the cold war, it is up to communication specialists to point out that the Soviets have not shown good faith at previous conferences, and that their real purpose is more likely to be to cause dissension among nations of the Free World.

Battles of interpretation among rival communication networks sometimes lead to "propaganda wars" in which the propagandist for one nation becomes primarily concerned with attacking the propagandist for another nation. This tends to be a waste of effort. The skilled propagandist keeps in mind the fact that the important audience is not his opposite number in some other country, but is rather the individuals or groups who are to be induced to take actions of a specified nature.

The view which has been presented here—that it is the principal function of international communication to report and interpret in accordance with a nation's foreign policy—may be contrary to ideas which are commonly held. There are many who think of the propagandist as the silver-tongued salesman who is able to break down even the stoutest buyer resistance by the brilliance of his presentation. Others may envision him as a missionary, who is able to convince unbelievers by the superiority of his dynamic faith. Still others imagine him as a shrewd psychologist, who somehow plays upon the subconscious of the hapless people in his audience until they blindly follow his will. All these popular stereotypes have a grain of truth in them, but can be seriously misleading if the grain is magnified to the size of a boulder. Ability in presentation *is* an asset to a propagandist; dynamic ideas *can*, under certain circumstances, be harnessed in the interests of policy; social science techniques *are* of value in reaching psychological objectives in general and in international communication activities in particular. But none of these represents a panacea.

An additional word about missionary propaganda may be required. At one time there were many who hoped that it would be possible, through superior communication techniques, to convert the world to democracy. One heard that what was required was a "Truth Bomb," a "Campaign of Truth," or a "Crusade for Freedom." Those who used these slogans often had in mind historical images such as the success of Christian missionaries in converting the heathen, the drive of Mohammedan armies toward victory and paradise as promised by the Koran, or the success of liberalism and democracy in sweeping across the civilized world in the eighteenth and nineteenth centuries.

If we look more closely at these dynamic ideas of the past, however, we will see that none of them were devised by national governments as instruments of policy. Instead, they had sprung from the minds of visionaries and philosophers, and had gradually increased in power until they were *adopted* as a means of policy by one or more states. Dynamic ideas are difficult to think up on order. Furthermore, at first they are likely to be considered subversive. One can imagine the storms of protest which would arise if the Voice of America commissioned a group of scholars to elaborate a new political, economic, or religious doctrine which it then proposed to foster in an effort to sweep communism from the the world.

If we survey international propaganda in recent times we find that there has been a steady trend toward increased factualness, a tendency to attempt to achieve goals far more modest than wholesale conversion. Only in certain relatively underdeveloped areas is missionary propaganda still powerful, and here the dynamic idea is that of nationalism. Unfortunately, nationalism in underdeveloped areas tends in most cases to favor Soviet interests and to make cooperation among the nations of the Free World more difficult. If a policy can be developed which will demonstrate to the peoples of underdeveloped areas that their national aspirations can, in fact, be realized more fully under a democratic system, then we will be well on the way to winning a significant engagement in the cold war.

The proper role which the propagandist should play in the formulation of foreign policies has been a subject of debate ever since the United States first embarked on a program of large-scale international communication. For the most part, the tendency of the propagandist has been to try to invade policymaking councils, while the reaction of the old-established government career men has been to try to keep him out. Actually, two separate and distinct functions are involved. These two functions may or may not be represented by one man or group of men, but if they are they must still be carefully distinguished. On the one hand, attention must be given to the psychological aspect of foreign policy, and this has very little immediate connection with the media of information. On the other hand, there is the operation of a complex communication network, which serves as one instrument of foreign policy.

At the present time, specialists in international communication are more likely to be admitted to policy-making councils than has ever been the case before. One reason for this is that these specialists have, as a rule, been more likely to be familiar with the social and psychological characteristics of foreign peoples than were old-line diplomats. They were thus more frequently able to give advice as to the probable effect of given policies and actions abroad. To an increasing extent, however, all officials concerned with foreign policy are coming to realize that taking into account the psychological aspects of what we say and do is not something that can be delegated to communication personnel exclusively, in addition to their other duties, but is part of the work of a large number of officials who are making decisions which will affect people abroad.

It is generally accepted that the communication specialist has an important function to perform in connection with the psychological aspects of foreign relations. It is less well understood that he has a vital but subsidiary function to perform in connection with economic and military aspects of foreign policy. A few examples will suffice to illustrate this relationship.

One of the major problems in the Free World is that some countries are weakened by poor health standards, backward agricultural methods, and a shortage of technicians. The United States and other free nations have endeavored to raise the level of hygiene and also agricultural production in these countries through economic assistance, through the training of local experts and bringing in foreign ones, and also by using the media of communication. Through films, pamphlets, and demonstrations millions of people in underdeveloped countries of the world have been taught better methods of taking care of themselves and their land. Work of this type, which the communication network performs in the interest of the effectiveness of the economic aid program, is less dramatic than much of the work devoted to developing, by direct appeal, favorable attitudes toward the United States, but it may be more important in the long run and may, in fact, more quickly create such attitudes as well.

In wartime the utility of official communication networks in the service of military operations is so obvious as scarcely to require comment. During World War II underground fighters were provided with useful information and were encouraged to persist in their resistance activity by means of radio and leaflets. Not infrequently, Allied communication networks were used to deceive the enemy— e.g., to make him think that attack would come at one point rather than another. Propaganda media have also been used to help take care of civilians in areas of military operations.

SOME SPECIAL PROBLEMS IN THE USE OF COMMUNICATION

International communication may be used in the service of general, specific, and middle-range foreign policies. Thus, some communications may be directed toward furthering the concepts of freedom and democracy in underdeveloped areas, others may be used to acquaint the world public with facts about a specific event, such as the invasion of South Korea by the Communists, while still others may be used in the service of middle-range policies such as the establishment of a South East Asia Treaty Organization.

The fact that international communications are used in connection with policies of all ranges creates a number of problems for the information specialist or propagandist. The most serious of these is that our general policies sometimes appear to conflict with our more limited or our middle-range policies. Thus our statements in support of semi-feudal governments in underdeveloped countries may be in striking contrast to our propaganda in support of freedom and democracy. Since these governments are often all that stands between millions of people and totalitarian communism, it is necessary to support them if time is to be gained for the gradual achievement of true liberty based on the development of healthy democratic institutions. To demonstrate this fact convincingly thus becomes one of the major problems of international communication.

Another result of the use of international political communication in support of policies of all levels of generality is that evaluation of the effectiveness of these communications—already extremely difficult—becomes even more complex. If communications are used in order to reach a very general psychological objective, such as furtherance of the desire to defend liberty, it will be difficult to make any definite statements about their effectiveness. If, on the other hand, they are used in an effort to increase the crop yield in a specific area, it is probable that their effectiveness can be gauged with relative accuracy. The first task in the evaluation of communication effectiveness, therefore, is to determine the precise objective which is being supported. If this objective is of a general nature, or even if it belongs to that category of objectives which we have designated as "middle-range," it is unreasonable to expect that a quantitative statement about the effectiveness of the program will be possible to make. Instead, reliance will have to be placed on a qualitative judgment.

Another general characteristic of international communications is their tendency to flow across national boundaries without the permission of the governments concerned. This is especially true of short wave radio, but even printed and other written materials or word-of-mouth messages do not always stop at the border for inspection. Propaganda and information thus have a subversive aspect, since, by entering without permission, they violate the exclusive authority which a government exercises over its territory. This subversive aspect can be mitigated by two facts. First, if the information is truthful, the value of truth is presumed to render the meticulous understanding of sovereignty and subversion irrelevant. Next, nations are in fact able to exercise a high degree of control over the official communications from those nations with which they enjoy friendly relations. The Voice of America would not beam to Great Britain any material which the British Government informed us was offensive in character, and the British Broadcasting Corporation would certainly observe the same restraint. A concrete example was provided not many years ago by the Republic of Korea, which objected to some of the ideas that were being disseminated in Korea by the United States and denied domestic rebroadcast facilities to the Voice of America by way of protest. This difference of opinion was, however, speedily adjusted.

While some control may be exercised over official international communications from friendly states, mass communications directed at unfriendly states may be subversive in character. We do not take into account the desires of the Soviet government in framing the content of our short wave broadcast to the Soviet Union. In an effort to maintain absolute sovereignty the Soviets have resorted to a systematic program of jamming Voice of America broadcasts as well as to a tight domestic censorship of printed materials. This censorship is, of course, maintained for other reasons as well.

In a democracy, private communications are usually subject to only a limited degree of control by the government, and serious embarrassment may be caused if these are considered subversive by friendly states. Not infrequently, for instance, individual copies of United States magazines have been barred by South American states with which we maintain friendly relations. The whole question is complicated further by the tendency of those who adhere to the principles of liberal democracy to deny that the state has the right to control the access of its citizens to ideas—no matter where these ideas originate. The doctrine of freedom of communication has, however, been restricted in many democracies by the principle that those who themselves would deny freedom of speech to dissenters cannot claim this freedom themselves. Nevertheless, the degree to which control of the flow of ideas is or should be one aspect of sovereignty remains a fertile field for disputation.

THE STUDY OF FOREIGN SOCIETIES

Both the policymaker who is interested in the psychological aspect of foreign relations and the communication specialist require voluminous information about foreign peoples. There is scarcely any datum about a foreign society which is not of interest to one of them and, incidentally, the fact that their research and intelligence requirements overlap so much is one reason why their functions have so often been confused. Any attempt to draw a line between information about foreign peoples needed by the communication specialist and that required by his colleague who is an expert on the psychological aspects of foreign policy is likely to be an arbitrary one. Nevertheless, certain differences in emphasis may be indicated.

The policymaker is primarily concerned with shaping our words and actions in such a manner that they will enable us to utilize the motivations of people abroad and will lead them to respond politically in ways we would welcome. Consequently, he is not equally interested in *all* behavioral phenomena abroad, but concentrates on what we may call politically relevant behavior—that is, behavior which is likely to have an appreciable effect on the attainment or non-attainment of our foreign policy goals. In a democracy, most adults are in a position to engage in politically relevant behavior at periodic elections. In between elections the number of people whose actions affect the relative power position of various nations becomes much smaller. Nevertheless, business and labor leaders, intellectual and religious leaders, and a substantial body of other people in addition to governmental officials are still in a position to take actions which we would classify as politically relevant. All these are of interest to the policymaker, whose business it is to shape the psychological aspect of foreign policy. He wants to know who is able to do what, and why he does it. To answer the "who" question the policymaker must be familiar with what we call the "power structure" of the society in question. To answer the "why" question he needs an immense amount of information about the history and social organization of the society as well as about the personal tastes, preferences and goals of the people concerned.

In a dictatorship, the number of individuals who are able to take politically relevant action is very small; it is ordinarily restricted to a relatively small number of political and military leaders. From time to time it is possible for larger numbers of individuals to make politically relevant choices, as in cases where there is large-scale hoarding of crops by the farmers, but for the most part the only function of the masses in a totalitarian state is to obey. Thus, an understanding of the behavior of those persons who *are* in a position to make important decisions becomes vital. It is for this reason that studies of the behavior of the *elite* in Communist countries have been so important. Also important is an understanding of the control system by which the political leaders manage to dominate the country— the secret police, the block wardens and the political commissars.

Lack of understanding of the limited political role of most individuals in a totalitarian state has led to a common belief which we may call the "democratic fallacy." This is the tendency to believe that the masses are most important politically than they are, that if they wished they could rise and overthrow their political masters. Another result of the "democratic fallacy" is a tendency to believe that the principal criterion by which to evaluate the importance of a propaganda audience is size, and a failure to realize that an audience of one man who can act is more worth addressing than an audience of a thousand who cannot. At the outset of World War II certain Allied propagandists appealed to the German people to "overthrow Hitler and end the war." This approach was soon discarded, as it was realized that the Germans were in no position to overthrow Hitler even if they wanted to. Under certain conditions, of course, it may be useful to gather a mass audience with the expectation that at a later date they may be in a position to act even if they cannot do so at present.

While the psychological adviser to political decision-makers is likely to concentrate on the study of politically relevant behavior abroad, the communication specialist is more likely to focus his attention on communication behavior. By this we mean that he must be familiar with formal and informal communications networks. He must know what types of people have radios and when they listen to them, which newspapers are read by intellectuals and which by farmers. He must also be familiar with patterns of rumor dissemination and must know how to present information so that it will be passed from mouth to mouth with the greatest ease.

Communication patterns differ markedly from society to society. In general, rumors and word-of-mouth communication are more trusted sources of information in totalitarian societies, while the officially controlled press and radio are viewed with suspicion. In democratic countries the reverse sometimes tend to be the case. When the armistice was declared in the recent Korean war, American troops who first heard the news in the form of rumors refused to believe it until it was confirmed by the Armed Forces Radio. The North Korean and Chinese troops, on the other side of the line, tended to believe news only when they *did* hear it through the grapevine.

DOMESTIC CONSTRAINTS AND OPPORTUNITIES

Although the task of calculating in advance the probable effect of our actions on various groups throughout the world is a difficult one, and the problem of understanding man's political behavior is formidable indeed, these are not the most serious impediments to the use of psychological expertise in attaining foreign policy objectives. Advances in social science techniques enable us to study individuals and societies with far more precision than before, and the rapidity with which information can now be gathered from remote corners of the Free World often makes it possible to learn about reactions to our policies very quickly and to make adjustments where necessary. The problems we have referred to so far are serious, but they are being overcome more rapidly than another problem—that of domestic constraints on the freedom of action in foreign policy. Several of the principal domestic constraints on our freedom of action in this field may be mentioned by way of example.

If we had to concern ourselves *only* about the behavior of people abroad, it would be easier to shape our actions according to sound psychological principles than is in fact the case. Actually, we must ordinarily give equal or greater weight to the way the American public behaves. As a servant of democracy the government official cannot take any action, even if it is manifestly in the national interest, if it is impossible to obtain sufficient political support for this action. For instance, the sudden termination of American lend-lease to Great Britain at the end of World War II tended to have an unfavorable effect on relations between the two countries. Specialists within the Department of State, who were concerned with evaluating the probable effect of this American action on the British people and government, counseled a policy of gradual termination. They advised that it would by psychologically more sound to give the British government a longer period in which to adjust to the loss of this substantial economic aid. Nevertheless, the domestic political situation made it necessary to economize. Domestic demands for economy overrode the advice of the area specialist and resulted in the immediate termination of lend-lease.

Another aspect of the domestic scene which makes the use of psychological expertise more difficult is our traditional distrust of official propaganda. For many Americans, propaganda is an underhanded form of activity and interferes with the right of the individual to make up his own mind. This distrust of propaganda, and of the people who make a business of conducting it, has been a perennial problem for those who have had to go to Congress each year and request funds with which to conduct our international information activities. It has also contributed to a situation where the top governmental experts in international communication have had to spend as much time defending themselves as in pursuing their professional activities. As more and more Americans come to realize that international propaganda is not necessarily reprehensible either in the means it employs or the ends it pursues, it is likely that the psychological aspect of our foreign policy will receive increasingly competent attention.

Even if propaganda were fully accepted as an instrument of policy, however, the fact that the government does not control private media of information in the United States would still impose severe limitations on the freedom of action of the official propagandist. The Voice of America could not misrepresent conditions within the United States even if it were expedient to do so, since accounts carried by the American press would be available throughout the Free World as well as to the governments of nations in the Soviet orbit. The uncontrolled character of the media of information in the United States, combined with the tradition that the taxpayer should be informed as fully as possible about the activities of his government, makes it difficult for our official propaganda media to achieve surprise and to ensure the best possible timing of disclosures. Those who are concerned with the psychological aspects of policy and with the government's international communications network, therefore, must be constantly aware that they do not enjoy a monopoly when it comes to informing foreign peoples about American plans and actions.

Domestic constraints may make the life of the American psychological adviser and propagandist difficult, but at the same time domestic conditions in the United States represent his greatest asset. While political leaders in totalitarian states are ordinarily fearful lest foreign observers discover the truth about conditions in their countries, American policymakers have ordinarily found that the facts about life in the United States are in the last analysis the best justification for American policies. Communist and Fascist states commonly enforce a direct or indirect censorship on information leaving their countries; the United States has spent millions of dollars to bring people to the new world so that they could see our way of life for themselves. The U.S. Government has also attempted to increase the freedom with which private media of information circulate throughout the world. Totalitarian states attempt to suppress criticism within their own borders and try to prevent criticism of their policies originating in other countries from being heard by their own people. The American government, on the other hand, cannot be shaken by criticisms coming from without, because it is almost impossible to find a major criticism of American policy which has not already been advanced from within the United States and aired in public discussion.

Domestic constraints on the manner in which the psychological aspect of American foreign policy is taken into account are thus more than balanced by the opportunities afforded by domestic conditions. It is part of the task of the psychological adviser to take into account not only what he knows about the social and psychological characteristics of the other peoples, but what he knows about his own society as well.

THE CHALLENGE OF NEW WEAPONS

In this discussion of the psychological aspects of foreign policy we have had little occasion to refer to the way in which psychological objectives vary in war and peace. The differences between the problems of taking account of the predispositions of foreign individuals and groups in wartime as opposed to peacetime cannot be dealt with adequately within the confines of this paper. In wartime, psychological objectives are stated more readily than in times of peace, partly as a result of the fact that people at home are then more likely to accept propaganda as an instrument of foreign policy, partly because of the strong feelings of righteousness which flourish generally in wartime, and partly in consequence of the fact that the supreme aim of winning the war provides a deceptively simple formulation of middle-range goals. We shall not pursue this elusive subject, however. It is perhaps more important to conclude this essay with a question pertaining to developments in the field of unconventional weapons.

We do not know whether thermonuclear weapons, or other weapons of similar destructiveness, will ever be used in a future war, but we can be quite sure that if both belligerents should have the will and the opportunity to employ them without restrictions the amount of destruction would be greater than the world has ever experienced before. Because this devastation would be so incomparably greater than anything we have previously seen, our past experience casts only a dim light on a future in which thermonuclear weapons play a role.

Predictions about policies and aspirations during and after an unlimited war are beset with enormous hazards. It seems likely, however, that the sheer destructiveness of thermonuclear weapons would lend an air of triviality to many of the policy calculations which have occupied statesmen and military commanders in past wars. We cannot give answers at this time; we can merely raise questions. How will the surviving populations in the affected countries behave in view of the possibility that devastating attacks might be made or repeated? Will they continue to obey their governmental authorities? Will they heed whatever warning the enemy might get across to them? Will organized social life break down altogether? The past provides us with few guides to help answer questions such as these.

Similarly, if any government ever decided to exploit the psychological potential of the threat of thermonuclear developments in its peacetime foreign policy, the implications of such a course of action are at present quite unpredictable. It is certain, however, that these implications would dwarf the psychological aspects of past weapons developments. Again, more questions than answers come to mind. Would it be possible to use a thermonuclear capability to increase the seriousness of a diplomatic ultimatum? Or would the fear aroused by such measure defeat its ends? Would it be possible for any government to present the hazards of thermonuclear developments in so impressive a manner as to rally world opinion against the countries with the most advanced science and technology in this field?

Of one thing we may be certain. The rapid increase in the destructiveness of available weapons will not overshadow their psychological aspect. Rather, the role which hope, fear, despair, expectations regarding the future, and other forces within individuals and societies play in influencing political behavior will tend to increase at the same time that man's mastery of destructive power increases. Ability to command even more massive forces in the external physical environment, rather than dwarfing the importance of the psychological aspect of foreign policy, presents us with new and more challenging problems in the understanding of man's behavior.

VIII
PSYCHOLOGICAL ASPECTS OF THE BLOC ECONOMIC OFFENSIVE IN LESS-DEVELOPED COUNTRIES*

THE SHIFT IN SOVIET STRATEGY

In the global power contest between East and West probably the most striking shift in Soviet strategy during the past decade is that which emerged in the less-developed countries of Asia, Africa, and Latin America. The initial calculations which led to militantly aggressive policies in these areas and the fomenting of revolutions in Asia until the later years of the Stalin period have been replaced by a strategy of providing temporary and tactical support to non-Communist, nationalist regimes and assiduously promoting the association of the U.S.S.R. with the aspirations of the less-developed world.

In a carefully orchestrated series of diplomatic, cultural, propaganda, and economic moves, the Kremlin has sought initially to gain international respectability and following this to insinuate its influence in areas considered weak links in the "capitalist-imperialist" system. Tactically, appealing offers to expand trade or provide credits for development or modernizing the armed forces are advanced as opening wedges from which the bloc hopes to establish beachheads of influence within a country or region. Such influence is used to encourage anti-Western neutralism in foreign policy and to aggravate existing "contradictions" and "antagonism" within the non-Communist world, whose industrialized powers are described as already weakened by the erosion of colonial empires. Against a background of growing Soviet power and the desire to avoid moves which would provoke a nuclear war, this softening-up process in the less-developed countries seeks to create conditions in which the victory of communism, viewed as historically assured, can be expedited. Toward this end, the less-developed countries have a twofold significance in the Soviet scheme: (1) a reduction of their economic ties with the major Free World powers is viewed as useful in hastening the crisis of capitalism and victory of socialism in the West; (2) some of the less-developed countries may themselves be ripe for socialist revolution.

The shift to a policy of correct state-to-state relations would in itself have constituted a remarkable change in Soviet policy. Yet the Kremlin's leaders apparently deemed that something more dramatic

---

*This chapter was prepared by Doris S. Whitnack, Chief, Bloc International Economic Activities Division, Office of Research and Analysis for the Sino-Soviet Bloc, Department of State.

was necessary to make credible Moscow's protestations of peaceful intentions and its newly found brotherly concern for the independence, welfare, and national aspirations of its poorer Afro-Asian neighbors. Criticism of Western aid fell on receptive ears, but still created little or no positive influence for the bloc. Attempts to claim credit for such aid as resulting from the postwar gains of world communism and its competition with capitalism were similary inadequate to achieve Soviet goals.

With the achievement of political independence, new regimes in these countries faced increasing pressure to translate their new freedom into international status and domestic welfare. Both required economic development and the symbol *par excellence* became rapid industrialization; in virtually no case were the domestic resources equal to the task. In this environment, the U.S.S.R., as the world's second largest industrial power, could hardly create the image and influence it wished to foster while leaving to the Western allies a virtual monopoly of such an important field as foreign economic relations.

Despite considerable internal debates about the need to retain scarce resources within the bloc and the wisdom of bolstering bourgeois regimes even temporarily, a new string was added to the Soviet diplomatic bow in 1954 as an economic aid agreement was signed with Afghanistan and the offer of a steel mill to India caught the imagination of the entire Asian subcontinent. Probably no other single aid project—bloc or Free World—has ever received such widespread publicity. The next year Western efforts to reduce tensions in the Near East were answered by large arms credits to encourage Nasser's strong anti-Westernism. To gain further publicity for the new look in Soviet diplomacy and cater to the desire of the Asians for status, Khrushchev and Bulganin toured Asia with the full resources of the Soviet propaganda machine trained on them. Catering to the desire of leaders for prestige and international recognition, invitations were issued to visit the U.S.S.R. A series of trade and aid offers climaxed the stay of the two Soviet leaders in each country. The exchange of high-level visits with flattering red-carpet treatment in Moscow as a prelude to economic agreements has remained a prominent psychological element in Soviet tactics. By mid-1961, 26 Free World countries had accepted bloc commitments for $5–6 billion in assistance, and a far larger number had expressed readiness to expand trading relations. Bloc probings to expand economic ties are continuing at a rapid tempo and bid fair to remain an important tool of foreign policy despite the recent Sino-Soviet polemics over the correct strategy for dealing with national bourgeois governments in less-developed countries.

RECEPTIVITY IN LESS-DEVELOPED COUNTRIES

Despite the undoubted contribution of assistance and trade toward improving the bloc image and influence in less-developed countries, most of the leaders in these countries recognize the political content of Sino-Soviet economic blandishments and profess some wariness about heavy involvement. What, then, are the elements of receptivity which Moscow has successfully exploited in expanding its economic offensive?

The so-called revolution of rising expectations which has supplanted the formerly widespread fatalism and resignation to a life of disease and poverty has forced all governments to give priority attention to economic development. The complexity of the problems involved and inadequacy of domestic resources create strong pressure for a policy of accepting aid from all sources provided no obvious political conditions are attached. If bloc aid is refused, the nearly inevitable gap between performance and aspirations is used by opposition groups as an effective club with which to beat the government in power as both inefficient in solving domestic problems and as subservient to the West.

The political ambitions of individual leaders can also be an important factor affecting receptivity to bloc initiatives. To be courted by a great power makes good publicity for the head of state and creates an impression of international status for the individual involved. Conclusion of a large aid agreement can be publicized as evidence of a leader's ability to bargain advantageously with a major power. At a slightly lower level, officials may view acceptance of bloc aid favorably in the hope that additional projects carried out under their ministry will build up their personal record and improve their competitive position vis-a-vis domestic political rivals.

The intense nationalism which characterizes the political scene in most less-developed countries often manifests itself in a neutralist foreign policy. In the economic sphere, the establishment of closer trade and aid ties with the bloc is often regarded as essential to demonstate this neutrality. The Soviets couch their argument for such policies in terms of the need for countries to assert their independence and to balance relations between East and West. Opponents of expanded economic relations allegedly seek to weaken neutralism and make the less-developed countries pawns in the "cold war."

Receptivity to credits for bloc arms and related technical assistance stems in part from the general desire to obtain the military trappings of a modern power. Most typically, however, the major arms agreements with the bloc have been made under circumstances which encouraged tensions in the Free World, and a Western alternative comparable to the bloc offer in magnitude or types of equipment was hence not available. Once such ties have been established on a significant scale, further arrangements tend to follow from the need for spare parts, ammunition, replacements, etc., and the fact that personnel have been trained to use bloc equipment.

Bloc and local Commnunist or front group propaganda organs harp endlessly on the theme that Western aid and private investment impinge on sovereignty and seek to maintain dependence; emotionally charged labels such as "neocolonialism" appear repeatedly. By contrast the bloc is pictured as seeking mutually advantageous trade relations and offering aid free of all strings and for whatever types of projects the country wants or needs to achieve economic independence. Programs are dramatized by inclusion of some major projects such as the Aswan Dam, and offers of other key undertakings are often timed and framed to undercut or exploit problems in aid negotiations between a Western country and a less-developed country.

While credits rather than grants are generally offered, a good face is put on this policy by presenting it as a more businesslike arrangement and more dignified than "handouts" for political purposes. To preserve an aura of goodwill, however, the generosity of bloc terms is emphasized, with particular attention given to low interest rates and the possibility of repayment in commodities. Economic justifications, technical problems, and future accounting checks are not raised, and negotiation of the initial aid commitment ordinarily proceeds smoothly and rapidly.

As time passes and more countries accept bloc aid without clearly damaging results, the remaining targets tend to be less inhibited by fear of ulterior bloc motives or unfavorable Western reactions. With some element of wishful thinking, examples of Soviet economic pressure for political purposes, as in Yugoslavia or Finland, are dismissed as special cases and large credit offers which were made conditional on disengagement from the West have generally received limited publicity. Increasingly, even anticommunist groups have been beguiled by the half-truth that development promotes stability and welfare, so that regardless of the bloc's motives, its aid weakens the appeal of communism and should be welcomed. Moreover, lack of detailed knowledge or sophisticated understanding of Soviet strategy combined with local pride, encourages false confidence in the ability of inexperienced governments to deal with the more subtle approaches to penetration represented by economic and technical assistance. On the more cynical side, flirting with the bloc is often prompted by a conscious attempt to secure more aid or better terms from the West. And should such involvement prove ill-advised, governments probably feel that they can count on the West to come to the rescue.

Attitudes toward bloc trade overtures tend to be dominated largely by economic considerations on the theory that the magnitudes involved seldom raise the immediate spectre of dependence or significant bloc political leverage. On the domestic scene, governments which see their immediate position menaced by accumulations of surpluses are often not inclined to give much weight to the longer term and less direct political implications of expanding bloc trade. Western caveats are suspect as being politically and economically self-serving in environments where trade issues have commonly become a subject of anti-Western attacks. Business groups, however, tend to feel that trade can and, in principle, should be divorced from international politics. The contacts and economic gains from expanded trade are assumed to promote understanding and goodwill between countries and thus contribute to world peace. Virtue thus reinforces a popular notion of necessity which argues that the bloc's more rapid growth than the industrial West gives it vast potential as a market, while opportunities for expansion of sales in the Free World are developing slowly.

ATTITUDES AND POLICIES ENCOURAGED BY BLOC AID AND TRADE

Once their economic overtures have been accepted, the question still remains as to how these are used by the bloc to create or strengthen attitudes and policies useful to itself. There is first the negative aspect of disparaging Western economic systems, impugning the motives behind Free World aid, and generally exploiting the legacy of resentment from earlier periods in an attempt to exacerbate relations between the industrialized and less-developed countries of the Free World. As a minimum, recipients of aid from the West are told they need feel no gratitude since the donors have "an historic duty to return some of the loot they have stolen." According to Khrushchev, "they are giving crumbs of what they have plundered . . . giving a kopek and trying to obtain a ruble profit out of it." Soviet spokesmen point out that the profit motive does not exist within the Socialist countries and, unlike the U.S., there are no surpluses that have to be unloaded abroad to relieve domestic depressions. Such assertions are a prelude leading to the conclusion that bloc aid represents an "unselfish contribution to the liberation of mankind from want, exploitation . . . colonialism."

In a variety of specific ways bloc programs are alleged both to be free of "neoimperialist" defects and to serve the national interests of the recipient. In the latter case, the Soviets hope to turn some of these interests to their positive advantage by encouraging foreign policies favorable to the interests of the U.S.S.R. and domestic policies that will create a more favorable environment in which bloc and local Communist interests can work to expedite the transition from the existing "nationalist revolution" stage to the "Socialist revolution."

In the current strategy of coexistence, competition in the economic sphere is a cardinal theme. Communist ability to produce an abundance of the sinews of national power has already been demonstrated, but efforts are now also being directed to catching up with or surpassing the West in a variety of nonstrategic goods. This image of rapid growth is utilized by the Soviets to encourage other countries to follow their model. Falsely, yet often effectively, they claim that only 44 years ago they were nearly as backward as today's under-developed countries. Their system is thus made to appear more effective than that of the allegedly devitalized West in rapidly converting feudal economies to modern industrial societies. Moreover, the Communist system is presented in terms of a scientific method whose success is historically predetermined. It thus appeals to those seeking fast, guaranteed solutions to complex problems and the presumed security of being associated with the wave of the future (the "bandwagon" theme).

Communists also have an asset in common misconceptions about Western economic and social systems. Virtually ignoring the institutional changes and welfare achievements of more than fifty years, large elements in the less-developed countries tend to think of "capitalism" in terms of the abuses which accompanied the early industrialization of Western Europe. Since Western economic systems are often viewed as lacking an authoritative, integrated, socio-philosophical ethic and even a clearly defined economic blueprint, they thus appear to be intellectually unsatisfying to the educated elites of less-developed countries. Among the latter groups a considerable number favor approaches to economic development which they label "socialism." As in various other areas, semantic confusion serves communist interests since the Soviet bloc describes its own system as "socialism" and, despite basic differences, tries to exploit superficial similarities. By contrast, while the U.S. gives large amounts of aid to support government economic activities abroad, it is philosophically opposed to socialism, and in principle emphasizes the desirability of a private enterprise system.

With the emphasis on speed and industrialization, the Soviets support planning which allocates a large role to the state sector and to the extent possible minimizes private enterprise. Virtually all of their aid goes to public projects in an attempt to encourage government ownership of key sectors of the economy, such as communications and transport, fuel and power, and heavy industry. There is also some evidence that within the public sector the bloc supports projects which enhance the prestige of local officials with views favorable to the bloc and looks with less interest on projects under ministries headed by anticommunist officials. By making large aid commitments quickly for programs extending over a period of several years, the Soviets can sometimes pre-empt significant projects or advisory positions for bloc aid programs, leaving those of lesser impact for the West. Large multi-year commitments also produce important psychological gains. These are followed up with publicity at each stage of implementation (signing of general aid agreement, survey stage, contracts for individual projects, start of construction, etc.). It is often difficult to determine whether a press release refers to a project under a previous credit or is a new commitment for additional assistance. This has helped to create the impression of far greater aid and more active implementation of programs than is actually the case.

Major emphasis in the bloc effort is given to technical services and training activities, with the extentive contacts they afford. For practical reasons, bloc personnel engaged in such work abroad have seldom done overt proselytizing, but they nevertheless serve a purpose far beyond their immediate technical job, namely, familiarizing people in the less-developed countries with bloc products and methods of work and subtly creating a favorable impression of bloc achievements. To stress the claim that bloc aid activities involve partnership and equality, projects are not run by bloc personnel but by a national of the recipient country, with bloc technical personnel in subordinate positions. Sometimes such personnel remain for a while after completion of the project, but, again in line with the "independence" theme, a point is commonly made of training local people to run the facilities themselves. This is done partly in the recipient country, but large numbers of students, officials, and technical personnel are also brought to the bloc for training in universities, factories, military installations, etc. The potential for impressing these people and affecting their views on a broad range of problems, as well as creating stronger ties is clear, particularly since most of them have no direct basis for comparing political and economic conditions in the bloc with those prevailing in the U.S. or Western Europe.

Since trained personnel in the recipient countries is usually very limited, such people often occupy a position of relatively greater individual prestige and influence than their counterparts in industrialized countries. As such, their potential value to the bloc is considerable. Until recently, professional and technical training came almost entirely from the Free World, but large-scale bloc programs are creating a substantial pool of people who will be accustomed to using bloc products and methods of operation. These technical assistance activities provide opportunities for promotional work which complements but far exceeds the possibilities open to trade missions.

Of special significance, particularly in newly independent states with inexperienced government personnel, is the bloc campaign to install advisers and even operating personnel in key ministries (planning, communications, finance, interior, education) where they can influence policies and administration to the benefit of the bloc. Technical assistance to the armed forces offers possibilities for penetration which are possibly even more dangerous in view of tendencies toward political instability in many less-developed countries.

An important tactic in the economic offensive involves fanning prejudices against foreign private investment, which is linked with colonialism and exploitation. Trade and aid are both used by the bloc to encourage nationalization moves, which tend to create frictions with the companies and their governments, reduce current Western influence, and create a climate unfavorable for new investors who would help perpetuate so-called bourgeois capitalism.

Bloc concentration on industrialization and related activities could be explained by the local appeal of such projects and the relatively greater bloc aid capabilities in these fields as compared with agriculture (excepting, perhaps, large dams involving a complex of development activities). The possibility cannot be ruled out, however, that the Soviet view further urbanization and a growing industrial proletariat as encouraging class struggle and providing fertile ground for developing Communist converts among workers recently removed from the authority and security of traditional family and village ties. This is not to say that rural areas are neglected by the Communists, but only that their campaigns in such areas, while exploiting socio-economic frustrations (i.e., agitation for land reform) have thus far utilized mainly other tactics than economic aid. However, as bloc experience in tropical economics grows, some expansion is likely in assistance for state farms and in technical assistance supporting changes in rural institutions modeled along Soviet lines.

In catering to national pride and aspirations for status symbols by giving aid for whatever projects a country wants, the Soviets can ignore the concept of balanced development which the West considers essential. Since the bloc would have much to gain by distorting soundly conceived programs, it must be assumed that it deliberately does so to the extent that is possible without revealing its hand. Unfortunately, the task is facilitated by the fact that sound programs often must contain unpopular features while projects of low economic priority are sometimes strongly desired by a country and yield highly satisfying psychological returns. This is not to say that most bloc projects are absolutely uneconomic, but rather that they sometimes divert scarce local resources to less than optimum uses.

In discouraging such activities as well as counseling a more moderate pace of development with an overall plan of investment which avoids undue inflation, the West is considered negative or unsympathetic and subjected to Soviet charges of foot-dragging to maintain profitable markets and cheap sources of raw materials.

Fundamentally the West is attempting to promote economic growth and social progress and is, willy-nilly, associated with existing political institutions if not particular regimes. When aspirations remain frustrated, moderate local governments favoring extensive economic ties with the West are discredited. The bloc position is far easier since Moscow can disavow all responsibility, arguing that the bloc has tried to provide economic help within the existing politico-economic framework, and lack of adequate economic growth only proves the validity of its contention that failure is inherent in a non-Communist system.

In the foreign policy field, the bloc economic offensive has, as noted above, a minimum objective of encouraging less-developed countries to assert their independence from the West under the banner of neutralism. Even if such a stance were truly impartial, it would constitute some gain to the bloc as a weakening of Western influence and an opening wedge for the bloc, which has hitherto had very limited contact with many of these countries, particularly those with colonial backgrounds. One of the important appeals of this bloc tactic of extending aid on a significant scale to unaligned countries has sometimes been characterized as "making neutralism pay."

Credits from the bloc—particularly those for military equipment and training—have been employed by the bloc to aggravate conflicts among Free World nations and induce neutrals to adopt policies favorable to the bloc. Large arms assistance to Egypt in 1955 and economic assistance at the time of Suez are a case in point. In other instances economic support has served to underwrite anti-Western policies which the country could ill afford to have risked without Soviet backing. The existence of bloc economic support (though not necessarily all in aid form) has strengthened Castro's hand in carrying out violently anti-U.S. policies. In such cases bloc political support, backed by economic agreements, enables the Soviets to pose as the champion of the less-developed countries, especially against members of Free World alliances on international disputes they consider crucial to their interests. The Soviets commonly take advantage of the aura of good feeling accompanying conclusion of an aid agreement to have inserted in the ensuing joint communiques an endorsement of their position on a variety of unrelated international issues such as the nuclear test ban and disarmament.

Efforts have been made through large aid offers to bribe states committed to Free World alliances—Turkey, Iran, Thailand—to leave such alliances or at least to void agreements giving military base rights to the West. Such overtures have been unsuccessful, but the blandishments are repeated periodically if only because they create pressure on pro-Western governments and raise demands on the industrialized members of the alliances.

Soviet aid is also used, sometimes fairly subtly or indirectly, to promote regional groups which are strongly anti-Western. Thus in situations where extensive direct bloc initiatives would be suspect or resented, the prestige of leftist leaders of groups hostile to Western interests may be enhanced through Soviet attention and major aid commitments in an attempt to strengthen their bid against more moderate rivals within the group. Some aid project offers have also been designed to orient the economy of the potential recipient toward a neighboring state with a pro-Soviet bias and hopefully to encourage its association with a grouping the bloc anticipates can be utilized to its advantage regionally and to back its positions in international forums.

THE PROSPECTS FOR DIMINISHING PSYCHOLOGICAL RETURNS

It is clear that in Khrushchev's eyes the economic offensive has yielded substantial returns to the bloc. It would be equally clear from the facts, even if Khrushchev had not expressly so stated, that aid programs are not profitable in an economic sense; thus the additional gains anticipated are in the politico-psychological area. To the extent that the bloc can sell the ideas noted above, it can consider its investment profitable. There are, however, a few problems which the Communists have only started to face and which suggest that the law of diminishing returns may well set in with regard to impact and influence to be gained from aid.

Bloc aid programs are still relatively new in most countries. Before long they will tend to be taken for granted, and the maintenance of an impact effect will tend to require ever larger outlays. This could well incur or strengthen resistance within the bloc from groups which already oppose foreign aid.

That little friction has developed with countries which have accepted aid is partly due to the fact that implementation of projects beyond the planning or survey stage is quite limited. As construction proceeds on a wider scale, the opportunities for disagreements, mistakes, misunderstandings, etc., will multiply. Excuses on the grounds that the bloc is new in the field will no longer carry weight. Some degree of disillusionment will inevitably result from initial overselling. In Iraq, for example, bloc aid was confidently expected to assure the success of a major development program which has hardly moved off of dead center nearly 3 years later, and the Russians could become a convenient scapegoat for the widespread popular disappointment. Elsewhere the speed with which initial Soviet aid agreements are concluded and the early arrival thereafter of survey personnel have created an exaggerated impression of Soviet efficiency which must already be waning in those areas where headlined agreements have still produced small tangible results.

Bloc rocket and space achievements have built up a generalized prestige for Soviet science and industry which Soviet aid programs have not entirely sustained in a number of particular instances. For example, a prestige export like airplanes has been widely recognized as inferior to Western models in design and operating efficiency. With respect to the petroleum industry, both drilling and refining, Western-trained personnel in less-developed countries have expressed considerable disdain for bloc equipment and technology. Over virtually the entire range of industrial machinery and equipment Soviet models are accepted as functionally adequate and even welcome because of the price and payment terms involved, but there is widespread recognition that the designs involved are commonly only a slight variation of a U.S. or Western European model of a decade or more ago. Growing familiarity with such items raises doubts about the vaunted superiority of the Soviet industrial system and the claims that its achievements have been due entirely to its own efforts.

Repayment experiences on credits (very limited to date) may well dash some of the satisfaction over having secured a "bargain" from the Soviets. Most countries confidently expect to meet their obligations in local commodities, hopefully those frequently in surplus. However, the Soviets are not committed to accept such goods, many of which have low priority in Soviet plans, and in any case the price is open to debate. If such leverage is used, the limited meaning of "stringless" aid will be exposed.

One of the most important problems arising for the Kremlin will be increasingly difficult choices between sides in disputes of Free World countries with one another (e.g., Afghanistan and Pakistan) or sometimes with a member of the bloc (India and Communist China). Goodwill built up through an extensive and expensive aid program can be lost overnight by a political position favoring an adversary in a dispute or even a rival for regional leadership (Nasser and Qassim). While it is sometimes possible to straddle the fence in these cases, this tends to create resentment and suspicion from both sides. As a minimum, such equivocation weakens the association of the bloc with national aspirations, an attitude which has been assiduously cultivated in campaigns combining unqualified endorsement of key political objectives with aid and trade agreements. It is also almost inevitable that the bloc will increasingly face a problem well known to the U.S., namely, resentment among aid recipients when one country feels that it is not getting as generous treatment as another less deserving country. Such jealousy can arise with respect to amount of aid, types of projects, prices, or annual repayment negotiations.

One of the greatest problems, however, arises from the basic conflict of long-term interests between existing non-Communist regimes and local Communist parties. Current tactics which involve subordinating the latter's interests usually promote at least the immediate foreign policy goals of the Soviet state and may even improve the local standing of the parties. This improvement can sometimes be utilized to inject Communists into some key positions in the government and to move the party closer to its assigned goal of gaining control of the national liberation movements. For such success, however, Moscow would have to pay the price of alerting the rest of the world to the Soviet interpretation of its pledge of noninterference in internal affairs which typically accompanies or is an integral part of economic and other agreements.

To date the renunciation of revolutionary action by local parties has not, as a practical matter, been very costly since very few of them have been in a position to make a serious bid for power. However, strong measures against a domestic party, such as Nasser's jailing of local members and the resulting acrimonious exchange between Cairo and the Kremlin, have undoubtedly been embarrassing to Khrushchev.

In the recent Sino-Soviet dispute, aid to bourgeois regimes was an important point of controversy. While differences were at least outwardly compromised, Khrushchev will henceforth be under greater pressure to show more positive political dividends from Soviet aid programs than mere anti-Westernism on the part of the recipients. Moreover, Moscow may feel less free to restrain opposition activities of local parties lest they shift their support to the Chinese side of the submerged but by no means settled dispute on Communist ideology and strategy in less-developed Free World countries. To the extent that they respond to these pressures, the Soviets are very likely to find their economic overtures viewed with greater skepticism and their aid operations subjected to closer surveillance. In such a climate Soviet development of goodwill and influence would be substantially more difficult than heretofore, particularly if the major Western powers themselves present an image of dynamic growth and an expanding Free World trade system within which the less-developed countries are able increasingly to show progress toward their own economic goals.

IX

PSYCHOLOGICAL TENSION IN INTERNATIONAL CONFLICT [1]

The discussion of psychological conflict in the preceding chapters has pointed out that the Communists' psychological efforts take on many forms, use a host of operating mechanisms, and have a variety of specific objectives depending upon targets and conditions. Yet, can one find a common denominator which might help bring these myriad facets into sharper focus? Granted, the ultimate goal of Communist psychological efforts is to promote the spread of communism. To achieve this goal the Communists may be said to have adopted a grand strategy aimed at inducing acute neurotic anxiety in their opponents. For its part, the West ought to prevent anxiety from infecting its societies, for neurotic anxiety, like dry-rot, could contribute to impelling the free peoples of the world to deterioration and then collapse.

Unfortunately, the Communists enjoy certain advantages in exploiting anxiety for their selfish purposes. This century has been aptly described as the "age of anxiety." It is characterized by great complexity, cultural disunity, and instability; most important, it is an age of rapid change and colliding cultures. The entire world is reverberating with momentous revolutions. The quickened and heightened pace of advanced societies has led to the frequent appearance of symptoms of mass neuroses. Researchers who recently studied the population of a compact residential area of New York City found that over 75 percent manifested definite anxiety characteristics. [2]

The emerging nations of the world are painfully restructuring their societies to accommodate new values and institutions as the old ones are destroyed. In this process millions of people, who almost instinctively followed a centuries-old set pattern of living, now must make an increasing number of individual decisions and choices; just as important, they must assume responsibility for their selections. Considering the magnitude of their problems, it is little wonder that they tend to feel a painful uneasiness of mind.

Anxiety often stems from facing the unknown and the seemingly unbeatable. It may occur when a person recoils from a threat to values essential to his existence, to his sense of being, and to his

---

[1] This chapter was prepared by Dr. Ralph Sanders.
[2] Isadore Portnoy, "The Anxiety States," *American Handbook of Psychiatry*, edited by Silvano Arlete, N.Y., Basic Books, 1959.

identity. One may become aware that he is about to be totally committed in a conflict—frequently not of his own choosing. He exhibits symptoms reflecting feelings of uneasiness, apprehension, foreboding doom, and perhaps even of going to pieces. Most important, the victim feels a sense of *helplessness* in the face of these various levels of threat. The impending situation appears to be so awesome as to be unsolvable by any actions which individuals or groups may choose to take.

It is helpful to distinguish between anxiety and fear. When one experiences fear, one does not necessarily see the threat as inevitably damaging his sense of being or his essential values. More important, one might still be relatively objective about evaluating the threat and acting in terms of this evaluation. A good soldier, showing fear in battle, nevertheless recognizes that he can reduce the risk of injury to himself by bringing into play his intelligence and training. Thus, if man only fears, he remains capable of devising adequate responses to cope with the threat. In contrast, when anxiety strikes, the individual not only sees the threat, but feels helpless in grappling with it.

We can speak more analytically perhaps if we separate what we might call healthy anxiety from neurotic anxiety. Healthy anxiety is looked upon as a normal phenomenon and it can act as a beneficial stimulant in human motivation. Healthy anxiety induces one to summon his resources to meet, to master, or at least, to endure a threat. Accordingly, courage, which is an expression of self-realization and development of the inner self, can be summoned to meet a challenge. Neurotic anxiety, on the other hand, inhibits such self-realization, prompts irrational behavior, and forces one to escape the unknown. In short, neurotic anxiety is fear in search of its cause.

The anxieties of the Free World societies are susceptible to exacerbation by the Communists. This is made possible by our very democratic way of life which produces a highly self-analytical people. Recall the tons of printed material purporting to be examinations or exposés of nearly every facet of our national life. Hence we frequently feel unsure of the explanations and interpretations of our way of life. We constantly are questioning basic concepts. Unmerciful, self-inflicted criticism, without an objective appraisal of both assets and liabilities, undermines faith in oneself.

Furthermore, the cold war and the threat of atomic annihilation cause added anxieties. Some in the West say openly that they feel that they are unable to save themselves from the impending holocaust. The attitudes of certain vocal scientists and intellectuals toward the atomic bomb reflect this feeling of defeat.

The editors of *Time* have made perhaps an apt description of these feelings of both shame (caused by overbearing self-criticism) and helplessness (partially induced by anxiety).

122

The possibility of civilization's total destruction is usually cited as one of the great factors contributing to anxiety in the U.S. But there is a strong suggestion that The Bomb is merely a handy device, welcomed almost with relief, for the release of anxiety and guilt that have little to do with the subject as such. For many Bomb worriers, it seems to be a true phobia, a kind of secular substitute for the Last Judgment, and a truly effective nuclear ban would undoubtedly deprive them of a highly comforting sense of doom.[3]

Clearly, it would be to the interest of the Communists to push the West into a state of mass neurotic anxiety. On the day when the West feels totally helpless before communism, the victory of the Sino-Soviet Bloc would be assured. Whether the Communists direct their psychological campaign along military, political, or economic lines in any geographic area, the ultimate aim is identical—paralysis of the enemy which can be hastened through mass anxiety. To the extent that Pavlovian tactics are used, they are made to order as anxiety producers.[4] By simultaneously preaching or following seemingly contradictory lines, the Soviets seek to baffle the enemy. Once confused, the enemy can be more easily stripped of will. It is not an accident that the Soviets rattle the nuclear saber at the same time that they mouth disarmament and peaceful coexistence. If the West feels helpless in understanding the Communists, how can it mobilize its resources effectively to challenge them?

Soviet conduct of the "nuclear" cold war illustrates this point. The "nuclear" cold war is the power struggle tied to threatened nuclear attack and takes the form of a series of maneuvers designed to make political capital out of high energy weapon systems (atomic warheads, missile delivery systems, etc.). It is like a dynamic chess game in which the players constantly introduce powerful technological chess pieces such as improved warheads, missiles, and guidance devices. The maneuvers resemble somber, simulated warfare in which the Soviets use high-energy systems to achieve political ends without actually firing these weapons. In this contest, the Communists appear to be exploiting the increasing efficiency of violence to induce the opponent into such a state of anxiety that he is willing to capitulate. Of course, no one action will turn the trick; consequently, the Communists execute a series of actions over a long period of time seemingly calculated to create anxiety. In short, they aim at a gradual weakening of the will to resist.

Thus, when Bulganin wrote to Prime Minister Mollet of France during the Suez crisis asking, "What would be the position of France had she been attacked by other states which have at their disposal the modern terrible means of destruction?", he sought to induce acute anxiety. Khrushchev strived for similar effects when, following the U–2 incident, he warned ". . . those countries that make their terri-

---

[3] *Time*, 31 Mar. 1961.
[4] See pages 49–50 for a discussion of this interpretation.

tory available for the takeoff of planes with anti-Soviet intentions—do not play with fire, gentlemen." The veiled threat of nuclear destruction against the U.S. in the Cuban crisis is another case in point. The Soviet approach has met with some success. Witness the attitude of Bertrand Russell, the renowned and controversial British philosopher, who believes that it is better to succumb to communism than to risk all-out nuclear destruction. Simply stated Russell says, "Better Red than dead." There can be little doubt that Russell and those who echo his sentiments suffer from a bad case of anxiety which is adroitly exploited by the Communists.

The psychological intent of Soviet economic aid also fits this general scheme. According to their way of thinking, Soviet economic aid to less developed countries will increase anxiety by creating a proletariat and an urban mass cut off from the security of established rural social relationships. Continued tensions in underdeveloped countries aid their cause. Once emerging countries realize the increasing gap between their accomplishments and their needs, frustration will follow. Without confidence in a better future, without a feeling of self-realization, without courage to do the difficult things that must be done, these people furnish a fertile breeding ground for communism.

The psychological efforts of the West are designed to help individual societies and their people to understand, to meet, and to overcome their basic conflicts. The goal is a reorientation of values as nations and individuals increasingly take responsibility for their actions. Free World countries should develop their capabilities to tap constructive potentialities. A positive psychology is needed both in our own country and throughout the Free World.

The American is constantly reminded that with him rests the future of the world—peace or war; prosperity or famine; the welfare and literacy of the last, most remote village in the Congo, Tibet, or Laos. He is faced with the choice of meeting his demanding destiny in a psychological state of either despair or confidence. He can either surrender to neurotic anxiety or marshal his inner resources to overcome his problems. He can either thwart Communist exploitation of his anxieties or lose control of his future. He either can set an example for free men everywhere of a knowledgeable, resolute fighter or a bewildered, anxious pawn. Taken as a whole, the Free World's destiny will, in a large measure, depend upon its state of mind.

SUGGESTIONS FOR FURTHER READING

1. Allen, Robert L., *Soviet Economic Warfare*. Wash., Public Affairs Press, 1960.
2. Atkinson, James D., *Edge of War*. Chicago, H. Regnery Co., 1960.
3. Aubrey, Henry G., *Coexistence, Economic Challenge, and Response*. National Planning Association, Wash., 1961.
4. Barrett, Edward W., *Truth is Our Weapon*. N.Y., Funk and Wagnals, 1953.
5. Cantril, Hadley, *The Politics of Despair*. N.Y., Basic Books, 1958.
6. Daugherty, William E. and Morris Janowitz, *A Psychological Warfare Casebook*. Baltimore, Johns Hopkins Press, 1958.
7. Holt, Robert T., *Radio Free Europe*. Minneapolis, University of Minnesota Press, 1958.
8. Holt, Robert T. and Robert W. van de Velde, *Strategic Psychological Operations and American Foreign Policy*. Chicago, University of Chicago Press, 1960.
9. Kalijarvi, Thorsten V. and associates, *Modern World Politics*. N.Y. Crowell, 1953.
10. Katz, Daniel, *et. al.*, *Public Opinion and Propaganda*. N.Y., The Dryden Press, 1954.
11. Kovner, Milton, *The Challenge of Coexistence*. Wash., Public Affairs Press, 1961.
12. Lasswell, Harold D., "Psychological Policy Research and Total Strategy," *Public Opinion Quarterly*, Winter 1952-53.
13. Lifton, Robert J., *Thought Reform and the Psychology of Totalism*. N.Y., Norton, 1961.
14. Linebarger, Paul M. A., *Psychological Warfare*. Wash., Combat Forces Press, 1955.
15. North, Robert C., "Peking's Drive for Empire; The New Expansionism," *Problems of Communism*, Jan-Feb. 1960.
16. Nove, Alec, *Communist Economic Strategy; Soviet Growth and Capabilities*, National Planning Association, 1959.
17. Sargant, William W., *Battle for the Mind*. N.Y., Doubleday, 1957.
18. Speier, Hans, "International Political Communication: Elite vs. Mass," *World Politics*, April 1952.
19. Strausz-Húpe, Robert, William R. Kintner, and Stefan T. Possony, *A Forward Strategy for America*. N.Y., Harper, 1961.
20. Szunyogh, Béla, *Psychological Warfare*. N.Y., William-Frederick Press, 1955.
21. Welton, Harry, *The Third World War*. N.Y., Philosophical Library, 1959.

INDEX

Eisenhower, President, and psychological warfare, 40–41
cited, 14
Elite, importance, in totalitarian countries, 104

F

Fainsod, Merle, *cited*, 6
Foreign Information Service, 34
Foreign policy (*see also* international relations).
economic measures, 89
function of communication specialist, 97–98, 100–101
involvement in domestic affairs and, 91–95
Marshall Plan significance, 95–96
misconceptions in psychological aspects, 91–95
nature of goals, 84–85
new weapons challenge, 107–108
psychological considerations, 83–109
role of international communication, 87–88, 95–101
role of propagandist, 100
study of foreign societies as basis, 103–105
subversion as goal, 93
U.S. domestic considerations, 105–107
Foreign psychological operations, U.S. (*see* U.S. propaganda).
Front groups, international Communist, 27–31
Fulbright Act, 35

G

Germany, U.S. propaganda efforts in, 38–39

H

History, importance, 68–69
Hypnosis, use by Communists, 52

I

Ideas (*see* ideology).
Ideological conflict (*see* conflict, ideological).
Ideology, 6–9
characteristics, 7–8
drive for power and, 5
Imperialism, Communist meaning, 78
Inter-American Affairs, Office of the Coordinator, 33

Interdepartmental Committee for Scientific and Cultural Cooperation, 33
Interim International Information Service, 34
International Information Administration, 37–38
International Information, Division of, 34
International relations
power needed in, 85–88
role of military aspects, 89–90, 97–98
role of offshore military procurement program, 89
use of external and internal pressures, 86–87

J

Japan, U.S. propaganda efforts in, 39

K

Kennan, George F., *cited*, 5, 20
Khrushchev, Chairman N. S., *cited*, 71, 74, 76
Korean War, 39–40

L

Language in propaganda, 71–73
Leighton, Alexander H., *cited*, 5
Lenin, V. I., *cited*, 9–10, 23, 25
Less-developed countries
nationalism and neutralism, 111
psychological aspects of Soviet bloc offensive, 109–120
Soviet aid, 111–113, 119–120
Soviet views on interparty strife, 120
trained personnel, 115

M

Marshall Plan, 95–96
Marxian doctrine, 9–14, 17–18, 19–21
Mass neuroses, 121
Mass organizations, 27–29
Mead, Margaret, *cited*, 19
Military movements, importance in propaganda, 98
Military strategy and limited objectives, 16
Moore, Barrington, *cited*, 6, 12
Movie industry, role in propaganda, 66–67

Time magazine, *cited*, 123

U

United States Information Agency, 41–43
  and use of television, 43
  congressional relations, 46
  media employed, 42–43
  organization, 43–45
  relation to other agencies, 45–46
U.S. propaganda (*see also* propaganda)
  evaluation of, 46–47
  foreign operations, 33–47
  general character, 64–65
  in Germany, 38–39
  in Japan, 39
  meaning to American public, 106
  Post World War II, 34–36
  President Kennedy's task force, 47
  private aspects, 65–67
  program, 40–41
  psychological value, 61–69

U.S. propaganda—Continued
  role of American public, 124
  uncontrolled character of information media, 106
  World War II, 34

V

Voice of America, 34, 42
VOKS (All-Union Society for Cultural Relations with Foreign Countries), 27

W

War, Communist view, 78–82
Warfare, psychological, 83–84
  effectiveness in military actions, 94–95
  semantic, 81–82
Weapons, 111, 123
Western psychological aims, 124
World Federation of Democratic Youth, 29–31

U. S. GOVERNMENT PRINTING OFFICE : 1965 O - 796-096

www.ingramcontent.com/pod-product-compliance
Lightning Source LLC
LaVergne TN
LVHW091307080426
835510LV00007B/391